THE HOME
WINE CELLAR

THE HOME WINE CELLAR

A Complete Guide to Design and Construction

by

Perry Sims

RUNNING PRESS

PHILADELPHIA · LONDON

9   8   7   6   5   4   3   2   1

Digit on the right indicates the number of this printing

Library of Congress Control Number: 2004104502

ISBN 0-7624-2084-7

DOLEZAL & ASSOCIATES

Concept and Senior Editor: Robert J. Dolezal

Production Manager: Barbara Dolezal

Cover and Body Designer: Hespenheide Design

Photoshop Illustrations: Jerry Bates

Illustrator: Ron Hildebrand

Indexer: Karin Arrigoni

Contributors:

Project Editors: Victoria Cebalo-Irwin

Consulting Editor/Text: Rich Binsacca

Writers:

Perry Sims

Rich Binsacca

Robert J. Dolezal

Photographers:

John M. Rickard

Jerry Bates

James Wilson

RUNNING PRESS BOOK PUBLISHERS

Editor: Lindsay Powers

This book may be ordered by mail from the publisher. Please include $2.50 for postage and handling.
But try your bookstore first!

Running Press Book Publishers

125 South Twenty-second Street

Philadelphia, Pennsylvania 19103-4399

Visit us on the web!

www.runningpress.com

TABLE OF CONTENTS

INTRODUCTION

A home wine cellar is a labor of love—a love of wine and the fine things in life, a love of fine woodworking and the richness of handcrafting, and a love of guests and entertaining.

Perry Sims is a master carpenter who specializes in wine cellar construction and is an avid fly fisherman. He plys his craft in El Dorado Hills, a suburb of Sacramento, California.

Wine culture and collecting wine may be ancient, but its present popularity is unmatched in history. New wineries seem to appear overnight. Close at home, builders, remodeling contractors, and homeowners create wine storage by converting closets and cabinets, installing appliances, and creating custom wine cellars.

Wine collecting is an avocation driven by passion for wine and wine culture. As your hobby grows, you will visit wine regions and wineries, taste new and unusual wine varieties, create food and wine combinations in your kitchen, and share your knowledge and experience with family and friends.

Let *The Home Wine Cellar* be your comprehensive resource for in-home wine storage. In its pages, you'll gain insight into what wine needs to age properly and how to balance your wine storage project with your budget. You'll see many options, from simple racks and wine furniture to elegant wine cellars.

Of all the lessons found in *The Home Wine Cellar*, it's most important to remember that every bottle of wine—regardless of its vintage or variety—deserves proper storage and care—a difference you'll come to taste, appreciate, and nurture.

INSPIRED STORAGE

For your collecting and tasting pleasure.

Collecting wine is a personal pursuit. Developing your tastes and building your collection are parts of an individual journey, though often—and fortunately—one you'll enjoy and share with other wine enthusiasts. How you undertake that journey reflects how you store, age, and display your wine.

Your ideal wine storage option may be a custom-built cellar in your basement or a refrigerated, insulated converted closet adjacent to your dining room. It could be series of self-contained under-counter chillers in various entertainment areas of your home, racking to display bottles of wine behind a bar, temperature-controlled space under a staircase, or a combination of wine storage options.

The style of your wine cellar makes a statement that reflects your depth of devotion to your hobby—an intimate experience of taste and appreciation.

What's truly ideal is what's best for you…and for your wine collection. As you consider how to store and age your wine, you will confront issues of convenience and capacity, learn about optimum wine storage conditions, scour your home for available space, develop budgets, reveal your passion, and marry form with function. Consider these elements early, and work to find a balance that leads you to an inspired solution worthy of your collection.

THE HOWS AND WHYS OF WINE STORAGE

Understand what wine needs—and what your wishes and desires are—to start creating an area in your home for proper, respectful wine storage.

Beyond very basic (yet critical) environmental factors detailed in Chapter 3, your wine needs and deserves your respect, and it will repay your efforts. Inspired wine storage solutions require true affection for wine. As you gain knowledge of the conditions that transform fine wines into great wines you'll nurture, enjoy collecting, and drinking.

Your enthusiasm must extend beyond knowing the "right" vintages or labels to pursue, the investment potential of a well-aged and stored wine collection, or the satisfaction you gain from displaying your wine for yourself, your family, and your friends. Such interests may play a part, yet they really only scratch the surface of a wine collector's appreciation.

A genuine fondness for wine involves an understanding of the arduous process in which it is made, including your discoveries of the sometimes subtle, often bold differences found between vintners and wineries. Along the way, you'll enjoy years of trial and winnowing to find your favorites, learn how to purchase and care for them, and build a collection to reflect your tastes and lifestyle.

The wine aging process is akin to restful hibernation. Subtle chemical reactions within the liquid transform the wine, softening hard edges and releasing its flavor.

Pairing fine wine with rich food brings out the best qualities of both. Training your palate by tasting wine will help you choose those bottles and dishes that complement one another.

Your journey of discovery will introduce you to wine culture, including food, travel, and the arts associated with wineries and vineyards. Even if you already know the difference between so-called table wine and properly aged vintages, and already take pleasure from both, you'll add new depths of understanding that allow you to treat your collection as a treasured and prized possession. You'll take pride in placing prized bottles in your cellar to later withdraw and enjoy.

Balance your passion for wine by understanding and respecting the real limitations you're likely to encounter as you plan a wine storage area in your home. Develop a keen sense for when and how frequently you'll enjoy wine as you plan the size of your cellar and the rate and quantity of your purchases. Match your passion for wine to your budget for wine storage. Develop your cellar over time; consider starting with a small stand-alone, under-counter chiller before moving on to larger projects and custom racking solutions.

The result will be an inspired storage solution that places the needs of your collection over other considerations.

Home Cellars and Storage

Home wine cellars or other storage options are ideal locations for a wine collection, regardless of size. Start with a healthy respect for what conditions wines require to age properly and how each wine and vintage differs, and be willing to provide them a space that suits their needs.

Most wines are meant for consumption within a year of its purchase. Such nonvintage wines are best suited for short-term—albeit still proper—storage. Sparkling wines, including Champagne, are ready to drink immediately and will deteriorate rather than improve with age (though good bottles can be held for many years at low temperatures that retard their aging). Rosés, table whites, and Beaujolais mature fastest, followed by table reds. Store them for a short time—occasionally up to a year—for they are best consumed soon after their release.

Quality white wines, such as Chardonnay and Fumé Blanc, may benefit from up to three years of aging prior to consumption, but rarely more. White wines lack the preservative tannins needed for long-term storage, and are the source of subtle chemical changes typical of red wines. The best Chardonnay and Sauvignon Blanc wines, for instance, commonly peak within four years. Great white wines may last another four before tailing off [see Aging and Serving Wine, page 159].

Fine red wines, by comparison, achieve their highest level of quality when they are aged under proper conditions for between three and ten years. Truly great reds are sometimes aged much longer, even for decades.

These red wines vary widely in their need for aging. Cabernet Sauvignons generally take longer to reach prime than quality Pinot Noirs and Zinfandels.

Wine favorites will accumulate in your cellar over many years. The single vintner's selection shown here spans bottlings from 1988 to 1993. The earliest of these bottles are at their prime and should be enjoyed now, while the latest vintages are only approaching their maturity.

Given optimum storage conditions, a high-quality Cabernet takes seven to ten years to age to perfection and will last another ten years before its quality starts to wane. Other red varietals peak in five to seven years.

Temperature and Humidity Control

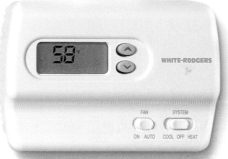

What are "optimum" storage conditions? Regardless of the wine storage option you choose, the critical elements are constant temperatures and average to slightly moist humidity.

Wine ages best at an unwavering temperature set in the range between 55° and 65°F (13° to 18°C) and 50 to 75 percent relative humidity. You can safely store the vast majority of a modern wine collection at the same temperature and humidity, whether red or white.

For wine to age, you must control the temperature of the cellar or storage location. In simplest terms, the warmer wine is, the faster it ages. Within limits, your wine will age more quickly at a steady, higher temperature than it will if the same vintage is stored at a lower temperature [see Chapter 2, pages 36–39, for more detail about temperature and humidity].

Thermostats for wine cellars require tighter control settings than are common for household use. The temperature within the cellar must stay constant within a degree for long periods of time.

Keeping the temperature constant is more important to proper wine storage and aging than your choice of a relative temperature setting within the preferred range. Always aim to achieve a consistent temperature within the optimal range when you build a space for wine. It's especially important when you convert cabinets, bookcases, and closets, but proper preparation of any storage space will make success more likely.

Climate-controlled wine storage requires adequate insulation and moisture vapor barriers; air-recirculated refrigeration; tight, durable door and window seals; and backup of electrical and refrigeration systems to prevent any lapses in service [see Backup Systems, at right].

Backup Systems

Mechanical systems in a wine cellar for temperature and humidity control will at some point lose power. Create storage environments that keep cold in and heat out with ample thermal mass, and consider a backup system should a refrigeration system mechanically fail.

Insulate and weather-strip doors to help maintain constant temperature and reduce demand on mechanical systems. You'll have less wear and tear, reduced likelihood of failure, and fewer maintenance issues.

North-side and middle-of-the-house locations minimize heat gain, while below-grade (or basement) locations provide natural, passive cooling, and the greatest level of thermal mass. Locate wine storage areas away from heat sources such as west or south-facing walls and windows, other appliances, and heat ducts; such sites tax mechanical cooling systems.

Consider paired refrigeration units, an auxiliary electric generator, or a battery backup power source to kick in when power fails.

MAKING A ROOM FOR WINE

Balance wine-storage requirements and your desired features to build a home for your wine collection that matches functionality with an appealing appearance.

Thermal mass from masonry walls and ceilings of stone and brick that absorb and retain heat help to maintain the constant temperature within a wine cellar.

Wine needs the right conditions to age properly and remain at its peak for full enjoyment. Each wine storage option has considerations you should recognize before you choose one. Look for solutions that meet your needs and those of your collection, whether it's a bookcase conversion, a self-contained wine appliance, or an elegant wine cellar with a custom racking system.

Consider the following issues and prioritize them as you plan a storage area for your wine collection:

- **Convenience.** Proximity and accessibility to wine often is a key factor when choosing a space for wine in your home.
- **Conditioned Space.** Climate-controlled environments are best for storing wine for more than two years and require building projects similar to a kitchen or bathroom remodel.
- **Capacity.** Large or potentially large collections are often best served by a combination of storage solutions.
- **Taste.** If you enjoy white and sparkling wines, a wine-storage appliance is the right choice. A climate-controlled cellar is the best solution for a collection of fine red wines that need to age properly.
- **Display.** Trade-offs exist when you combine storage with the desire to display your wine. Consider tinted, insulated windows in doors or walls.
- **Space Loss.** Converting a closet or basement means making sure you have other places in your home to store coats, books, board games, cleaning supplies, and holiday decorations.
- **Mobility.** Should you plan to move in two to five years, modular racking, stand-alone chillers, or wine furniture may be your best choice.
- **Budget.** Know your resources and plan within them.

Keep track of your collection with software to record your wine purchases and generate a wand-readable bar code label for each bottle. Store information about the wine's flavor, cost, origin, and improvement with age on your home computer.

CUSTOM WINE CELLARS

Are you ready to take the plunge? Beyond any doubt, a room devoted to wine is foremost in the plans of every enthusiast and collector.

Behind this heavily insulated glass door is an appealing custom wine cellar that holds more than 1,000 bottles for aging.

A custom wine cellar is the wisest investment you can make if you have a large or growing collection of wine selections and vintages that require aging and proper storage to reach their full promise. Giving the collection a proper space will add to your enjoyment of the wine itself.

A wine cellar adds value as a functional space and amenity of your home. While the purpose of a custom wine cellar is for your personal enjoyment while you live in the house, it also adds to the home's resale value; wine cellars are among the most popular features of new custom and luxury homes, and they are especially prized in older homes located in established, desirable neighborhoods.

Design and build a custom wine cellar specifically for your collection, taking into account your available space, budget, and the convenience of having ready access to quality wine. You can locate it nearly anywhere in your home—in an unused closet, a room corner, in a pantry, under a stairwell, or even in an attic—though some spots, such as basements, are better-suited environments than others [see Converting Space, page 26].

Each wine cellar requires adequate structural support for the racking and mechanical systems. It may also contain a small counter and a small amount of case, bulk, or bin wine storage. Its walls need proper insulation to maintain constant temperature, and it should have a continuous moisture vapor barrier to prevent condensation within its walls and hold its humidity. The cellar's door must be sealed with perimeter weather stripping and insulated to keep cool, humid air inside the cellar. And, of course, it requires special systems for refrigeration and humidity control, plus electrical systems for limited room lighting.

Finishing the wine cellar is next, most notably installing special racking. Racking should accommodate your cellar's dimensions and your collection; not all bottles are the same or can fit into standard, off-the-shelf wine racks. Other finishing touches include the choice of flooring, baseboards, crown moldings, lighting (only as necessary), countertops and cabinets (if applicable), door hardware, and other accessories.

Now you see it...and now you don't! When this display shelf is pushed back, it recedes into the fully stocked wine cellar behind it. Such features add interest to any home and are a fun touch that helps keep your collection secure.

Take note of cellar organization when you plan a wine storage room. Here, country flags help organize bottlings from different countries. A tasting table is used instead of counters to give more storage room in the wine racks, yet is ample for quickly opening and tasting a bottle before it is presented to guests.

Elegant Wine Cellars

Custom wine cellars typically reflect finish carpentry at its most elegant level. They are appointed with the highest grades of materials, hardware fixtures, system components, and aesthetic flourishes. An elegant wine cellar adds immediate value to a home and is a showpiece for the owners. It both stores and ages wine properly, but it also displays the collection in a manner that catches and holds the eye—an enviable meeting of form and function.

A custom wine cellar should accommodate between 600 and 1,000 bottles or more, depending on the collection, its usage or rotation rate, and its varietal contents. Even if you start with less than a few hundred bottles, you may soon exceed the cellar's capacity as your affection and enthusiasm for wine increases. A cellar that holds over 1,000 bottles leaves enough room for growth and rotation of well-aged wine, and it may provide cold storage for perishable items.

At the other end of the spectrum, a cellar that holds many thousands of bottles exceeds the needs of even the most enthusiastic collector. There's a practical limit to how much wine a family can consume, and aging fine wine acquired over decades only to discard or sell it when it passes its prime is a waste of the wine and your personal resources. Large cellars should be reserved for investment collections, rather than everyday, consumable ones.

Elegant wine cellars may feature arched niches with glass or mirrored shelves, polished wood or granite countertops, and vaulted stone or coffered ceilings that mimic winery tasting rooms. These cellars also reserve areas for different kinds of wine and varied bottle sizes, including custom racking for individual bottles, open bins for case quantities, and specialty racks for sparkling wine and magnums. Most have space within them to open wine and to store glassware.

What a wine cellar is not, however, is a room for entertaining, dining, or even prolonged tasting. At a typical temperature of 55° to 60°F (13° to 16°C), an ideal wine cellar is simply too cold for comfort. A tasting table, bar, or other seating area invites spending time in the cellar and raising its temperature—to the detriment of your wine. If entertaining is a primary goal, accommodate guests with a separate, adjacent room near the cellar.

Good design combines high-quality materials and thoughtful use of space. Achieve elegance on a modest budget by making sure your cellar serves both your wine's and your own needs. Some elegant cellars are modest to build, yet retain an appealing appearance.

Given its cool, slightly humid conditions, a wine cellar also serves as excellent storage place for fine furs—plan on a separate but also climate-controlled closet—and for cut flowers, fresh vegetables, and fruit. When it's finished, you'll discover what a nice room it is and use it more often than you thought.

Custom Racking

Wine cellars deserve storage racks, shelves, and bins designed and built specifically for your collection.

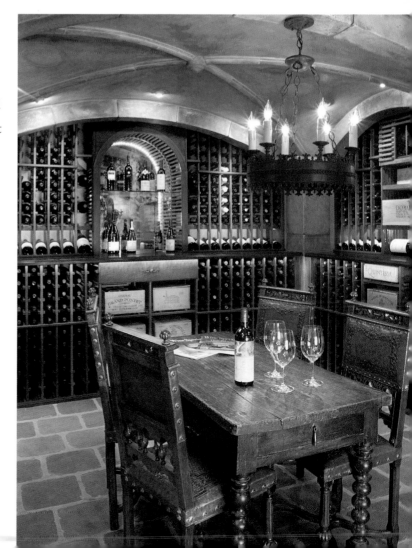

A faux-finished plaster cathedral groin ceiling and decorative paint help create the illusion of an underground cave in this home wine cellar. Mirrors in the niches make the room appear larger, and the cave allows both individual bottle and case storage in Bordeaux boxes.

Redwood is by far the most common material for wine racks. It is beautiful and naturally resists moisture damage, decay, and insect infestation. Redwood is easily cut, shaped, and fastened, compared to other materials such as pine or oak that are less forgiving. While perhaps more costly than other less-suitable woods, redwood remains competitively priced, and is the material of choice used by wineries for their racking systems.

Bottles held individually in racks should be snug and secure from vibration. The rack should hold the bottles nearly flat or slightly inclined with the cork submerged, so that the ullage—air bubble—rests near the middle of the bottle.

Bin racking stores bottles loosely on top of one another, often to save space. Remember, however, that bins make labels hard to identify, are more prone to breakage, and actually waste space if case quantities leave the bins partially filled.

Racks should also have space for upright bottles, such as for sparkling wines with pressure closures, and for screw-capped bottles. Screw-capped wine bottles lack corks to keep moist and air-tight, and they may leak when set horizontally. A growing number of wineries are switching to screw caps due to a shortage of quality cork material and problems with odor, or "nose," though these issues rarely occur in cellars with adequate temperature and humidity control.

Vertical racks, seen on both sides of the Bordeaux cases, are very efficient for storing large quantities of wine. Slant racks help identify an individual bottle, while its case mates are racked above or beneath the displayed label and are easily accessed.

Full-case Storage

An exception to the cautionary note about bin racking exists for full-case shelf racking. Make sure your cellar accommodates wine by the case for storage or display. Cases of wine hold the bottles in an upside-down position or nearly flat in the case of a wooden Bordeaux box. Each shelf holds one or more cases or boxes of the same vintage and label.

Avoid long-term storage of wine in cardboard cases. Cardboard cases will deteriorate in the humid conditions needed for an aging wine cellar, which may cause the bottles to break if left unchecked, and over time they become unsightly. Invest in wooden boxes and transfer bottles to them when you first store the wine in your cellar.

Butlers' Pantries

A small cellar or self-contained wine storage unit in a butler's pantry, usually adjacent to the home's kitchen, addresses both proper wine storage and issues of convenience. Most butler's pantries are equipped with a counter, a sink, and a wine-chilling appliance as well as open racks to temporarily store wine. With the kitchen and dining areas nearby, wine can be easily and quickly enjoyed.

A butler's pantry also can accommodate glassware and utensils. It supplements the functions of the kitchen and dining room with preparation areas, ambient-temperature storage, and intermediate-term wine storage, increasing its value to you as you cook and serve, as well as to your guests.

Because the wine in a butler's pantry is destined for immediate consumption and the space is smaller than the main cellar, plan for a capacity of between 100 and 350 bottles, including 30 to 75 bottles in a wine chiller. Wine in a butler's pantry cellar will rotate quickly, and it's meant to be enjoyed and replaced. For best results, the temperature of rack storage should be lower than 65°F (18°C) and experience minimal fluctuation. This limits the aging process and allows you to present the wine at drinking temperature.

A butler's pantry makes part of your wine collection visible and may include a glass-paneled door for display. Choose a door with dual-pane, insulated glass to reduce temperature fluctuation, and insulate the space's walls, floor, and ceiling.

A butler's pantry off a dining room is an elegant area for food preparation, silver and stemware storage, and—of course—a wine chiller to hold bottles for a short time prior to serving.

Special glasses suited to individual wine varieties can be stored inside the cellar itself or in an adjacent room. It's best to hang them from their stems or stand them upright, as seen at right, rather than place them bowl down on a shelf, as is the case for the front row of glasses below.

Glassware and Its Storage

Wine glassware is best stored outside your cellar. Keep glasses from collecting dust and allow air to circulate by hanging stemware upside-down. Glasses stored rim-down on a counter can trap stale air and affect the wine's taste.

The ideal glass for most red wines is about six to eight inches (15 to 20 cm) high, with a three-inch (75-mm) stem, a bowl three inches (75 mm) in diameter, and a capacity of between 10 and 12 ounces (296 to 355 cc). Many designs vary on this general theme. An open bowl allows the wine to oxygenate in the glass and develop flavor as it, in essence, ages before your very nose.

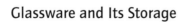

Doors and Cabinets

The tight-fitted, insulated door to your cellar is necessary to age and store fine wine properly. Each time you enter the cellar, the door allows cold air to escape; the longer it remains open, the more your cellar's temperature fluctuates. In turn, the refrigeration system must work harder and cycle more often, reducing its service life. Always strive to build a wine cellar large enough to allow you to walk inside and close the door behind you.

A standard, exterior-grade residential door is ample for most wine cellars. You should add perimeter weather-stripping to block air leaks from and to the room. Make a tight seal to hold cold air in the cellar, and pay special attention to where the door meets the floor. Consider wood, close-set marble tiles, or concrete to ensure a smooth surface and a tight door seal. Avoid carpeting in wine cellars.

With smooth floor finishes, install a sweep at the bottom of the door to seal the gap between the door and the floor, or use a spring-loaded weather-strip system. Such systems move down as the door closes and retract as it opens.

For ceramic tile or other rough-textured floors, install a raised threshold across the door opening extending less than an inch (25 mm) from the floor. A threshold creates a flat, even surface for the weather-stripping sweep and seal.

Cabinets in your wine cellar add to its elegance. Use a wine chiller or an insulated cabinet with its own refrigeration system to hold mature wines at slightly colder temperatures than the cellar as a whole and preserve their quality. Use standard kitchen cabinets to house wineglasses and utensils for opening and tasting wine before you remove it from the cellar.

A beautiful blend of function and form can be achieved with a thick, carved-wood door that conveys the theme of your wine cellar and its contents. Wood naturally insulates. The door jamb is tightly weather stripped, and it has a threshold to block air leaks.

CONVERTING SPACE

Turning an existing area of your home into wine storage can save construction time and is among the most economical of alternatives.

Converting existing space in your home into a wine cellar depends on what's available and whether it can be made suitable for wine storage.

Altering existing space may also require upgraded electrical systems to accommodate the wine cellar's refrigeration system or wine appliance. Consult a licensed electrician for expert advice. The conversion might also necessitate reinforcing the structural frame and flooring to handle the additional weight of the addition and the wine it contains—a typical bottle of wine weighs a bit more than two pounds (0.8 kg), and even a modest collection of 500 bottles weighs half a ton (453 kg) or more. These factors make a ground-floor site preferable to one on raised flooring or a second story. On the other hand, a basement site might require waterproofing to make it dry enough to store wine.

Converting existing space and furniture into wine storage is challenging, but it may still be your best choice. Be aware that you are attempting to "re-engineer" something for another, unintended use. This can require more effort, more compromises, and perhaps a larger budget than building a wine cellar or storage unit from scratch.

Basements

Below-grade or full basement areas are the top choice for wine cellars. A concrete, masonry, or permanent wood foundation is naturally insulated from the outside air, is cooled by surrounding soil, and provides ample thermal mass to limit temperature swings. Basements, being more naturally humid than above-grade areas, often require less mechanical humidity and refrigeration than an above-grade installation.

Your basement may already be a finished space, or you can finish it prior to installing your cellar. Basements can have natural light from light wells and casement windows as well as artificial light to brighten the area. A basement can accommodate space for your cellar along with a second area for tasting, dining, and entertaining.

It's best to start with a finished basement, complete with insulated walls, ceiling, and floor, lighting, and two points of egress such as doors and windows.

Above: This basement cellar incorporates within it a boulder found on the home's building site. Special iron frames mount to the stone with drilled holes and mortar. They support the wine racks that appear to float above it.

Opposite page: Racks behind a wrought-iron gate in an ambient-temperature room are suited to short-term storage of table wine intended for early consumption.

Bookcase Conversions

An antique icebox built with thick, insulated metal walls is a good choice for conversion into a wine storage cabinet suitable for use in a room with cool and steady ambient temperatures.

One attractive solution for wine storage is converting a bookcase. An existing built-in, or a piece of furniture that complements your home's decor, already uses space in the house.

Bookcases are best for short-term, low-volume storage. They are challenging to insulate and refrigerate. Use them to display wine you plan to consume within a year or so.

Add cabinet doors to open bookcases to protect the wine from light, and replace the shelves with wine racking to best utilize the space and hold the bottles securely. Remember that bookcases are subject to toppling, so anchor them to the wall or floor before filling them with wine.

Commercial Racking Systems

Commercially manufactured or off-the-shelf wine racks offer affordable alternatives to custom-made racks. Many options exist for these racks, with layouts, materials, and finishes that complement your home's decor, making it easy and convenient to store wine, either in a wine cellar or in an open, unconditioned space. Most standard racks are made to hold Bordeaux-shaped bottles (most red varietals) rather than Burgundy bottles (the majority of white varietals), sparkling wines, or other bottle shapes and sizes in your collection. Choose only wood racking systems of high-grade wood stock and quality craftsmanship. Commercial racking systems are the right choice for a tight budget and a small wine collection destined for near-term consumption. Custom racks, by contrast, make the best use of space and are designed specifically for your cellar's needs.

Closet Conversions

Closets are better conversion projects than bookcases. They are relatively easy to adapt to climate-controlled environments and can be insulated, moisture-sealed, refrigerated, and humidified. When sealed with a weather-stripped, exterior-rated door, they make an ideal environment for long-term storage of modest wine collections. The best closet choices are those deep enough to stand inside and close the door behind you.

While high in adaptability, closets offer smaller capacity—perhaps 300 to 600 bottles—and influence your collection's rate of rotation, temperature of storage, and pace at which you age your wine.

The primary advantage of a closet conversion is convenience. Many closets are close to kitchens, dining rooms, or entertainment areas. Show off your wine collection with an energy-efficient glass-paneled door, and add elegance with custom racking. If the closet is large enough, include a small counter to display or open wine in the cellar.

Understairs Storage

Deep, hollow understairs closets make good wine storage areas and create an attractive, interesting feature for your home. An understairs space also works well as either open-air racking or with climate-control. The best understairs locations occur where a wardrobe or storage closet has been enclosed. Add insulation and a moisture vapor barrier on the walls and ceilings.

Understairs locations have a few drawbacks. Their capacity may be limited, and footsteps overhead on stairs may vibrate the bottles in the cellar.

Below-Counter Storage

Convert the area under your kitchen or bar counters for wine racks or to accommodate a self-contained wine storage appliance [see Self-contained Wine Appliances, page 30]. Either is a welcome feature for a kitchen, dining room, or other area. Built-in storage optimizes an under-counter area for a limited collection of bottles destined for near-term use.

For ambient-temperature wine storage, renew or adapt existing cabinets to hold wine racks, and replace unused under-counter appliances with wood or steel wine racking, wine cabinets, or wine appliances that fits their dimensions. Off-the-shelf wine racks can fit into such spaces with room to spare, but they have less capacity than custom-built racks. They may also accommodate only certain bottle styles and sizes. They compensate for these limitations by being mobile, however, and you can take them out and move them elsewhere as needed.

An understairs cellar in a niche off a formal dining room brings a wine collection close for serving while protecting it from heat and light. The narrow insulated door with a stained glass inset into a deep alcove helps block daylight from reaching bottles stored on the inside walls of the cellar.

SELF-CONTAINED WINE APPLIANCES

If you are looking for a mobile, easy solution to your wine-storage needs, consider installing an appliance or a piece of wine furniture.

Wine appliances bring small wine collections to a kitchen or dining room. They can be used alone or in combination with larger cellars.

Self-contained or component wine storage, either as a unit built into furniture or cabinet, or as a stand-alone chiller, is a popular alternative to building a custom wine cellar or converting space. They typically provide conditions suitable for up to two years' wine storage. Many are small to midsized, plug-in appliances suited to kitchens, bars, dining rooms, bedroom suites, or butler's pantries.

Installing and using a chiller is simple. Like most appliances, chillers are delivered complete and ready to use. Remove the chiller from its packing, plug it in, set the temperature, and stock the racks with wine [see Installing a Wine Chiller, page 68].

Unconditioned self-contained wine storage units, on the other hand, often look like furniture. They conceal the wine in a handsome cabinet that may also double as a bar for tastings and other refreshments, and they frequently offer a place to store glassware, flatware, and wine utensils.

At the other extreme, self-contained wine storage solutions include modular, large-capacity cellars—complete with climate control systems, insulated structures, weather-stripped doors, and racks. They are delivered complete, or they may require some assembly, similar to that of a spa. They require an electrical source to run their refrigeration systems.

Built-In Units

Built-in wine storage units look as though they were custom-made, whether you install them under a counter with cabinets and other appliances or set them in a closet or a corner.

Wine appliances are also available in refrigerator-sized units, with the capacity for hundreds of bottles or even cases of wine.

Right: A built-in, under-counter wine chiller makes for convenient access. They can slide into bays made for trash compactors and dishwashers, or replace an existing base cabinet, and decorative trims match the units to your existing kitchen cabinets.

They often compare in volume, capacity, and expense to a custom-built cellar. Convenience of installation is their primary appeal, and you'll often find them in a kitchen beside a standard refrigerator or freezer.

Large-capacity, modular wine cellars are the next step up in size from refrigerated appliances. They come in a variety of sizes, and some can be customized to fit an available space. These units generally require a dedicated power supply, a stable base sized to the unit's specifications, and wall, ceiling, door, and rack component assembly. They economically deliver large-capacity, climate-controlled wine storage with a fraction of the effort and time required for a custom-built cellar or conversion project.

While built-in wine storage units may appear permanent, they have the added benefit of disassembly for moving—a distinct advantage over a built-in wine cellar. You can take them with you if you relocate.

Wine Appliance Pros and Cons

Self-contained wine storage has advantages and disadvantages. Few other options can match its convenience or economy. Wine appliances can be stepping stones to larger, custom-designed cellars or can house selections from your larger collection. They are convenient for holding white and sparkling wines at slightly colder temperatures than your fine red wines.

Self-contained wine storage also has compromises. Its storage capacity is limited beyond the number of bottles a unit holds. Few self-contained appliances have racks that can accommodate odd bottle sizes [see Custom Racking, page 52]. Many Chardonnay, Pinot Noir, Champagne, and other, larger-diameter bottles simply will not fit. Self-contained units are also subject to vibration, too-dry conditions, ambient light, and swings in temperature.

Wine Furniture

Stand-alone units that resemble buffet cabinets, media centers, wardrobes, or bookcases offer even more mobile short-term storage options.

Most stand-alone units are delivered ready to stock with wine. They can provide either climate-controlled or ambient-temperature storage. Wine furniture is a good choice for small-capacity, everyday wine storage and display.

With wine's increasing popularity, the options for wine storage furniture from which you can choose is likely to grow, matching just about any cabinet style, furniture form, or decorating scheme.

Like their built-in counterparts, stand-alone wine units are ready-to-use appliances. Their mobility allows use in many situations, indoors or out, bringing wine storage where you need it; some are mounted on casters for portability. Many chillers have veneer, stainless steel, or enameled finishes and tinted glass doors.

Refrigeration vs. Temperature Control

If you store wine in a standard refrigerator—even some economy wine chillers—be aware that you're placing your investment in less-than-ideal conditions. Refrigerators and many chillers draw in outside air and cool it; air within the unit exhausts to the outside. This continuous cycle of replacing warm, moist, stale air with cool, dry air dehydrates everything inside the unit—including your wine. As a result, the corks dry out, wine evaporates through the closures, and oxygen enters the bottle, accelerating aging.

Refrigeration systems specifically designed for wine cellars and quality chillers, by contrast, recirculate the air and condense moisture within the units, recovering it to maintain constant humidity. As a result, the wine ages and is preserved in a climate of appropriate humidity and temperature.

Fine furniture to store wine in a climate-controlled environment comes in many sizes and finishes.

CHAPTER 2

FUNDAMENTALS OF WINE STORAGE

Meet the requirements to age and store fine wines.

The basics of proper wine storage and aging apply to every type of cellar, converted space, and wine appliance—they are universal, scientific, and tested. Your wine collection's health depends on respect for these fundamentals.

Temperature is the most important consideration affecting the quality and enjoyment of all wine, and fine wines benefit the most from proper aging. If you maintain a consistently cool temperature in your cellar or other storage area, it will be a nurturing home for your collection [see Temperature, page 36].

Learn the things wine must have to age properly and achieve greatness. Make the time spent in your cellar a period of awe-inspiring transformation.

Other factors have an impact on wine quality but to far lesser degrees: humidity, light, vibration, oxidation, sedimentation. Pay attention to them, however, and you'll provide a setting in which your wine can mature and achieve greatness.

Understand what your wine needs; recognizing and comprehending its requirements are as much cornerstones of your wine cellar project as its walls, racks, and refrigeration system. Equipped with knowledge, you'll balance form with function as you design your wine storage.

TEMPERATURE

The best wine cellars have unchanging temperatures that either allow wine to slowly age, or somewhat cooler temperatures to hold mature bottles that are ready to drink.

The temperature in your wine cellar determines the pace at which your wine will age and, once it reaches maturity, preserve its quality. Cooler is better to a point, but the aging process stands practically still below 50°F (10°C). On the high end, a cellar set over 65°F (18°C) ages fine wines too quickly and damages older, more fragile reserves. Setting a temperature within this range determines the rate of aging for the wines in your cellar, an important consideration that in turn controls how fast you will rotate and consume your stock.

For most home wine collections of more than 500 bottles, a constant, regulated temperature of 57°F (14°C) is ideal and acceptable for the majority of varietals, vintages, and labels. At that temperature, a quality Cabernet Sauvignon typically needs seven years to reach its peak, and it will maintain its greatness for an equal span. Boost the setting to 60°F (16°C) for smaller cellars in which the wine rotates quickly or when you want to enjoy a fine, current-release Cabernet in less than four years. Whatever temperature you choose, keep it constant within one degree for best aging and preservation. Within the

Some thermostats use a probe in a dummy bottle filled with water to measure the wine's temperature, controlling a cellar's temperature.

recommended temperature range of 50° to 65°F (10° to 18°C), the consistency of the cellar is more critical than the actual temperature. Fluctuations of even a few degrees cause wine—or any liquid—to expand and contract.

Fluctuations in temperature oxygenate your wine. If, for instance, the wine warms to room temperature, then cools back down to 57°F (14°C), the wine will first expand, compressing the ullage, or air bubble. Then, as the temperature cools, it will contract, pulling room air with oxygen and carbon dioxide through its porous cork.

Proper aging is the slow, measured chemical change of the wine, and fluctuations in your cellar's temperature will damage a fine wine. Ideally, if the temperature remains constant, the wine will age steadily as a small amount of liquid evaporates through the cork to be replaced by an equal volume of air. Under constant temperature conditions, this process takes place very slowly, creating pressure inside the bottle that reduces the amount of fresh air that can enter the bottle and react with the wine. Whatever temperature you choose for your cellar, keep it steady.

Maintain your cellar's temperature with an airtight, insulated structure and ample thermal mass [see Thermal Mass, page 112]. Masonry walls, floors, and ceilings, whether freestanding or shared with another structure, provide the highest level of thermal mass. Use them in your cellar to help keep temperatures constant and extend the service life of your refrigeration and other mechanical systems. Seal all gaps in the cellar's structure with expanding foam, and fill wall, floor, and ceiling cavities with fiberglass batt or rigid foam insulation. Weather-strip doors and use insulated glass [see Planning and Building a Wine Cellar, page 89].

Thermal mass alone, however, simply maintains a constant ambient temperature. It needs assistance to create a specific temperature setting. Refrigeration systems and controllers are thermal mass' partners that deliver and maintain a set temperature. Choose a system that recirculates air within the cellar, rather than drawing and exhausting air and moisture outside the cellar, to help hold optimum humidity levels.

Bottle-probe thermostats are accurate measures of a wine's actual temperature. They may be slow to react to changing air temperatures that cool or warm the wine.

Effects of Heat on Wine

Heat is the enemy of fine wine, affecting both the aging process and wines' preservation. As wine warms (or ages), it naturally comes in contact with chemicals in the air, absorbing oxygen, nitrogen, and carbon dioxide, and creating complex chemical reactions that affect the wine's quality. Fine wine is meant to age this way, albeit slowly. A fine Cabernet vintage, for instance, requires four to as many as seven years to age properly and achieve its optimum flavor, color, and aroma. Accelerating that process by storing the wine in a warm cellar—or at room temperature—adversely affects each of those qualities. If you want to enjoy a well-aged wine, protect it from heat.

OTHER EFFECTS

Discover the effects on wine in your cellar caused by humidity, sedimentation, ullage, the volume of wine you store, light, oxygen, and vibration.

Humidity

Humidity is the amount of water vapor in the air, expressed in terms of a percentage of relative humidity. The amount of moisture air can hold varies with temperature. As conditions reach 100 percent humidity, water condenses from the air into its liquid form; the

Recording thermometers and hydrometers graph the changes in temperature and relative humidity within a wine cellar over a span of time ranging from weeks to months. They are especially useful for measuring changes in passive cellars and wine storage areas with ambient temperatures.

higher the temperature, the more moisture it requires to achieve condensation, or dew point. In a climate-controlled wine cellar, keep the humidity level between 50 and 75 percent. Humidity of 60 percent is optimal. Maintaining an even humidity level keeps corks moist from the outside—the wine itself moistens the cork from the inside—and slows the transfer of gases, oxidation, and evaporation.

Humidity also impacts the cellar's racking systems, wine labels, and other equipment, especially if it is too high. Humidity over 75 percent in a cellar with temperatures below 65°F (18°C) result in a moist, rainforest-like environment. Mold and mildew thrive to deteriorate labels, your wine racks, and cellar walls.

Control humidity with a self-contained refrigeration system that recovers or condenses moisture within the cellar itself; a separate humidifier (or dehumidifier) is occasionally necessary, though you should provide extra humidity in wine chillers and other small wine appliances used for short-term storage. This counteracts the drying nature of their refrigeration systems. Wine storage appliances that hold many bottles destined for long-term storage are usually designed to control temperatures and maintain optimum levels of humidity.

Sedimentation

Sediment is a normal feature of a finely aged wine, a sign that it has developed to a fuller potential in your cellar. Sediment forms as tannin and alum crystals precipitate with oxidation, gathering with other solid particles chemically formed as the wine ages. Moving an aged bottle may stir up its sediment and cause the wine to become cloudy; if this should occur, simply stand the bottle upright for a few days to settle it before serving. You can also riddle older bottles—give them a quick twist—as they age to concentrate any sediment they contain along a side of the bottle or its bottom, or decant them before serving [see Decanting, page 164]. Cloudiness also can be a sign of bacteria or yeast feeding on residual sugars in wine, and either will adversely affect its taste and smell.

Tartrate crystals are often mistaken for sediment but in fact are a naturally occurring result of chilling wine. The wine releases clear tartaric acid as it chills, forming crystals, most often in white varietals. Though they resemble small shards of glass, tartrate crystals are harmless. Some wineries cool wine before bottling to precipitate these crystals, then filter and remove them. Many vintners filter their wine to remove sediment, though purists believe that mechanical filtering degrades a wine's quality.

Careful decanting with or without a filtering sieve removes any accumulated bottle sediment from wine. The process also introduces large amounts of oxygen to the beverage, releasing its flavor and improving its taste.

Ullage

Ullage—the amount of air within the bottle—increases as wine ages. The wine lost is known as "the angel's share." You seldom see this effect in wines aged for two decades or less in ideal conditions.

Ullage is the air space within the bottle between the wine and the cork, often seen as an air bubble in bottles resting on their sides. As the wine ages, the liquid expands and contracts with temperature variations. These, in turn, cause wine to be pushed out and air drawn in through the cork. The amount of air may grow as some of the liquid is lost. Typically, wineries fill their bottles to their necks, and ullages that remain nearly constant over long periods of time indicate well-sealed wine that is aging properly.

If you find excessive air in a newly released wine, though, the bottle might have been inadequately filled at the winery. More likely, air has invaded the bottle or liquid was lost through a dry or faulty cork. The wine's quality and its value will be reduced.

For Bordeaux-style bottles (most red varietals), ullage below the shoulder should cause concern; for Burgundy style bottles that lack shoulders (most whites), avoid ullages greater than one inch (25 mm) below the cork.

Volume and Storage

The capacity of your wine collection helps determine the environment for aging. Because smaller reserves rotate faster, store them at temperatures up to 65°F (18°C) to accelerate their aging. Use lower cellar temperatures for large, long-stored collections with slower turnover and aging.

A tight-packed wine cellar has great thermal mass, but each bottle releases a bit of heat as the wine oxidizes during aging. Good air circulation to all of the bottles would help minimize variation and assure that each matures at the same rate.

Rack your collection properly. Place bottles on their sides, flat, or slightly tipped toward the neck, with the air bubble resting at the middle of the bottle, or at a slight incline with their corks immersed. Wet corks equal good seals.

By contrast, store screw-capped bottles upright; they can leak when placed horizontally. Screw-cap closures are increasingly popular for even very high-quality wines because they prevent spoilage due to faulty corks.

Individual bottle racks accommodate different-shaped bottles and display the wine for easy access. Provide diagonal, diamond-shaped, or multibottle bins and shelves to store quantities of the same label and vintage.

Vibration

Vibration becomes a concern when it's excessive or constant, stirs up sediment, or, in the worst case, breaks bottles. Minimize vibration with properly installed and anchored racks. Move, shift, or stand bottles only when necessary.

Vibration during shipping can make wine cloudy when you receive it. Allow it to settle and recover; bringing it slowly to cellar temperature. Make your cellar a haven free of vibration so your wine can reveal all its intended qualities.

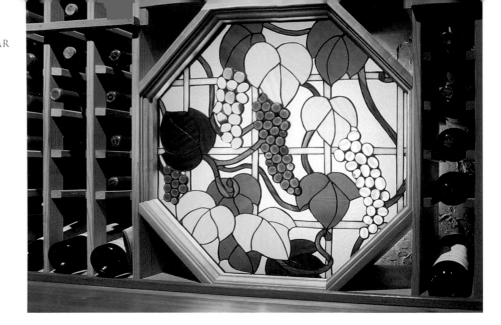

Simulate a window in your wine cellar by mounting a stained-glass panel in front of a cool fluorescent fixture. The result will be visually pleasing yet will protect your wine investment.

Light

Light, both as rays and as a heat source, can affect the quality of your wine [see Temperature, page 36]. Light rays—especially sunlight's ultraviolet rays—excite charged ions within the wine and hasten oxidation, speed up chemical processes, and cause premature aging. Dark-glass Bordeaux bottles effectively shield wine from light; cellars and wine appliances should have tinted glass doors and windows.

The best cellar is a dim cellar. Store wine away from windows, and provide only enough lighting in your cellar to find, open, and decant a bottle. Turn off lights when you leave. Use low-wattage and fluorescent bulbs that generate limited heat, and control them with dimmers to cast light where you need it. Consider

From left to right, Salmanazar, Methuselah, Jeroboam, magnum, standard, and split.

using motion sensors to ensure lights turn on when someone enters the cellar and shut off automatically, or control your lighting system with a timer switch.

Oxygen

Wine ages best with limited exposure to air. Oxygen causes chemical reactions that influence wine's taste, aroma, and color—a process similar to rusting. At best, an oxidized wine tastes flat; at worst, it becomes a vinegary liquid rich in acetic acid.

Store bottles with their corks moist to keep oxygen from entering your wine. At bottling, the ullage contains oxygen, of course, but it is quickly consumed. When all the oxygen is gone, a process necessary to aging begins, called reductive oxidation.

Large wine bottles take longer to age than smaller bottles. In identical storage conditions, a 1.5-liter (51-oz.) bottle takes roughly twice as long to mature as a 750-ml (25-oz.) bottle. Aging occurs even more quickly in half- or split bottles.

When any wine is stored for seven decades or more, its label will discolor and deteriorate. Limit these effects by controlling humidity within your cellar.

Deterioration of Labels

Cellars with excessive humidity and abrasive racking can make labels deteriorate. In extreme cases, they become illegible or detach from the bottles. Losing labels makes it more difficult to maintain a proper rotation of your collection.

Keep the humidity of your cellar below 75 percent and seal bottles with damaged or peeling labels in shrinkable plastic film—a covering that protects the label from stains. If necessary, add a dehumidifier, along with a controller. If your cellar is too dry, add a humidifier to increase moisture in the storage area.

CHAPTER 3

WINE RACKING SOLUTIONS

Choose racks suited to your space and collection.

Most wine offered for sale is meant for either immediate consumption or limited storage. Typically, even the best "production" Cabernet Souvignons and Pinot Noirs have four-year shelf lives, and the lives of white varietals are even shorter. These wines seldom benefit from aging but deserve proper care and handling. Enjoying such table wines allows you to display them in room-temperature storage, from simple off-the-shelf racks to custom racks designed for varied bottle sizes and shapes. Fine quality wines, by contrast, are designed for cellaring, aging, and mature consumption. Custom racking is usually the best choice for them. Most wine racks can be used in either refrigerated cellars or ambient-temperature spaces.

A modest cellar may store only 750-ml standard bottles, but larger collections should provide for bottles of every size, for bulk storage, and for wooden cases.

Regardless of whether you store your wine in a climate-controlled cellar or in your kitchen in a simple wine rack, choose racking that displays your labels as you might a favorite piece of furniture—as a measure of your pride, accomplishment, and good taste. Always store corked bottles snugly on their sides, horizontally, to keep their corks moist. Store screw-cap bottles upright, to avoid leakage.

EVALUATING THE SITE

While modern homes offer many choices for ambient-temperature wine storage, select one with minimal temperature variations. For true climate-controlled cellars, choices narrow.

This understairs wine cellar fills a niche with off-the-shelf, modular racks, uses an under-landing space for a wine appliance and counter to decant, and has another wall lined with a combination of bins and individual bottle racking.

Wine matures quickly in open-air environments. Plan to drink wine stored at room temperature within a few years of its vintage release to enjoy its intended flavors and aromas. You will have greater latitude when choosing open-air sites than for locations suited for a climate-controlled cellar, but always pick spots that protect the wine from temperature variation, excessive light, and vibration. Balance your desire to display the wine with the need for convenient access. These considerations also limit your choices when you select a location for a temperature- and humidity-controlled wine storage area.

Look seriously at both the surroundings found in various parts of your home and your storage needs; weigh the cellar's form and function with your needs as you choose a spot for your collection.

Surroundings

Consider locations for wine storage that blend in with or complement existing furnishings and decor, including a room's colors, textures, and styles and finishes, so that your wine reserve enriches the space. To protect the wine, choose a place with minimal foot traffic; jarring is less of a concern than bumping. A spot that intrudes too far into a room invites breakage.

Select an area where the wine can be seen and admired, but one that is free of heavy traffic.

If possible, place your wine collection near other storage and serving areas—by existing bars, counters, butler's pantries, or buffets. Consider multipurpose units that store wine and keep glassware, utensils, and other tools and accessories close at hand. Freestanding wine racks are available with optional tabletops and with built-in glassware storage, as are many built-in racks.

Finally, give your wine cache a fighting chance to reach its peak potential by avoiding storage locations in direct sunlight, next to heat sources—such as a kitchen's oven, range, or dishwasher—or prone to harbor food or waste odors, or areas with very low humidity.

Space Needs

The amount of wine you want to store—and rotate—in any racking system, storage cabinet, or true wine cellar will, in large part, determine its dimensions, final location, and overall design. For collections of up to 100 bottles, consider a bookcase, a wine cabinet, an understairs conversion, or perhaps use several smaller storage options in multiple locations.

A large wine collection can easily dominate a room's decor, and you may wish to consider designing the room to fit your wine collection. On the other hand, for a more subtle statement, look for opportunities to showcase only a few bottles at a time, keeping the bulk of your collection's reserve in another, more protected environment, such as in a garage, basement, butler's pantry, a converted closet, or another hideaway.

In addition to capacity, allow space for all the types and sizes of wine bottles you plan to store or display [see Bottle Sizes, page 61], and decide whether you will stock bottles of the same label, vintage, or variety together or individually.

Case shelves and horizontal bins add versatility and a visual break to the vertical racks for individual bottles in this wine room.

SIMPLE RACKING SYSTEMS

Off-the-shelf wine racks offer convenience, economy, and flexibility, but have the tradeoffs of limiting the amount of wine you can store and the sizes of the bottles in your collection.

Above: Modular wooden diamond racking for multiple bottles is a one-size-fits-all storage solution.

Below: Metal stackable racks for individual bottles.

Wine-racking systems run the gamut from simple, open-air wood racks to custom-designed furniture with built-in accessories, lighting, and innovative ways to display wine, and from off-the-shelf, modular units to custom racks. Well-planned wine storage and display systems exist to accommodate and complement just about any style, capacity, and budget. Learn the pros and cons of each type before making the choice of racking for your wine cellar or storage area.

Commercial Modular and Fixed Racking

Commercial, off-the-shelf wooden wine racks arrive disassembled with all the hardware and instructions necessary to put them together using basic skills and simple household tools. Metal rack systems, which offer a contemporary look and accommodate different bottle shapes and storage positions, are usually made in snap-together modules or shipped preassembled; accessories, including countertops and hangers for glassware storage, may have to be fastened to the metal racks once they are installed.

Ready-made wooden wine racks are available in either modular or fixed configurations. You can assemble modular systems to fit a particular space such as an undercounter area or a cabinet, or to convert a bookshelf to wine storage furniture. Each freestanding row or column is an independent module with either scalloped, horizontal rows or traditional vertical stands with racking for each bottle. The units fit together, enabling you to lay them out side by side or stack them to fit your location and capacity.

In addition to traditional racking that displays bottles neck-out, also plan to use display shelves (in which the bottles lie horizontally—and securely—across the shelf), waterfall and stepped racks, rounded corner display racks and shelves, and units made for volume bin and case storage. Use diamond-style or vertical bins, for instance, to stack bulk quantities of the same wine.

Many fixed racks feature furniture quality finishes, and they may also have built-in or add-on accessories, including doors, drawers, fixed or folding counters, tabletops, shelves, and hangers for storing glassware. To save space, some wine racks feature extra-tall or deep rows with space to stack two bottles instead of one. In such cases, choose units constructed of sturdy materials.

Once you find a style you like, choose racks made of materials that are a solid, high-grade lumber or a heavy-gauge metal, with racking at least 12 inches (30 cm) deep. Fixed systems and cabinets are freestanding as well, with sides, a back panel, and often a top enclosing the rack. They may also be stackable, with clips or other mechanisms to connect and secure the racks together. With either modular racks or fixed systems, always secure the racks to a wall with anchors into the wall studs to prevent them from toppling.

The ability to stack and customize modular and fixed wine storage units enables you to configure the racks to suit your collection's needs.

Conversions and Custom Racking

While choices abound in catalogs, furniture show-rooms, and even Internet sites, you should also consider kits or instructions for adapting the shelves of a bookcase, an entertainment center, or a china cabinet for wine storage [see Converting a Bookcase, page 50]. With a few well-placed stops or scallops that support bottles at their necks and near their bases, almost any built-in or freestanding shelf or cabinet can be customized to hold the wine in your collection. Or, you may build your own racking [see Building Wooden Racks, pg. 54].

After a lifetime spent as a china cabinet, this piece was found at a consignment store. It was altered into an ambient-temperature wine storage cabinet. The steps used to perform its conversion are found on pages 50–51.

CONVERTING A BOOKCASE

A bookcase in your home or one found at an antique store or furniture auction is easy to convert to wine storage for a room-temperature collection. Retain the existing shelves and outfit them with slanted holders to display bottles, or replace the shelves with racks especially made to hold individual bottles of wine.

Cabinets with glass doors keep your bottles of wine visible while reducing the amount of temperature variation experienced in a typical room. You can also convert open shelving, built-in bookcases, and entertainment centers to hold wine.

Choose a bookcase or cabinet with shelving at least 12 inches (30 cm) deep—14 inches (36 cm) is better—so that it will hold standard Burgundy and the longer Bordeaux bottles used for many white wines. Deeper cabinets are also more stable and unlikely to tip if you include pullout shelves. If you shop for a bookcase to convert, take a tall bottle along with you or measure the furniture piece's interior depth with a tape measure.

You'll need an electric drill with screwdriver bits, drill bits, and a hole saw bit; a saw; wood screws; a hammer and brads; sandpaper; stain; and varnish or latex urethane coating. Follow the steps shown to convert the bookcase to a wine cabinet.

Materials for One 12″D × 24″W (30 × 60 cm) Cabinet		
Neck Holder	**(1)**	1″ × 5½″ × 24″ (19 × 140 × 610 mm)*
Foot Molding	**(1)**	¾″ × 24″ (19 × 140 mm)*
Bottle Shelf Ends	**(12)**	¾″ × 1½″ × 11¼″ (19 × 38 × 286 mm)†
Bottle Shelf Spacers	**(24)**	¾″ × ¾″ × 11¼″ (19 × 19 × 286 mm)†
Bottle Shelf Facings	**(12)**	¾″ × ¾″ × 24″ (19 × 19 × 610 mm)†

*Length equal to interior bookcase width, less ¾″ (19 mm).
†Length equal to interior bookcase depth, less ½″ (12 mm).

STEP 1

Remove and reserve existing bookcase shelves and their mounting hardware. If you plan to convert existing shelves to bottle slant shelving, note the side clearances needed to clear bottles on each side. Divide the remaining width equally, allowing at least 3¾″ (95 mm) between the centers of each bottle location, and mark the positions on the neck holder and foot molding.

STEP 4

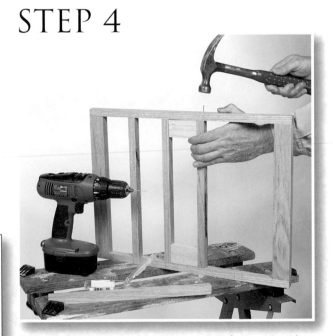

For individual bottle racks, make an outer frame using the bottle shelf ends and facings fastened with wood screws. Use a spacer block, 1½″ (64 mm) wide, to set each bottle shelf spacer, drill pilot holes, and fasten them with brads.

STEP 2

Use an electric drill mounted with a 1" (25 mm) hole saw bit to drill neck holes along one edge of the neck holder. With a saw, rip the length of the neck holder through the center of the neck holes. Fasten it with wood screws set through the back of the shelf, set back 2" (50 mm) from the shelf's edge.

STEP 3

Fasten the foot molding to the front edge of the shelf, then rip wedge strips and mount them along the molding, making cradles for the base of each bottle. Stain and varnish the wood to match the existing shelf finish, then remount the shelf. Repeat for each slant shelf.

STEP 5

Make additional individual bottle racks as required. Stain the wood to match the existing cabinet finish. Allow the stain to dry completely before applying varnish. When the racks have dried, sand lightly and apply a second coat.

STEP 6

Hang bottle racks in the cabinet using the existing mount holes, or drill new mount holes using a ¼" (6 mm) bit with a stop. Insert shelf-support hardware, available at home centers and hardware stores.

CUSTOM RACKING

When only the best will do or your needs dictate, build custom racks for your wine. Plan carefully to gain the greatest volume of storage for a given area.

Bring on the wine! A combination slant rack and vertical individual bottle rack permits display of one bottle and storage of up to a case in the spaces above and below it. Note how the rack sections are doubled in the curved section.

While many models and options exist for off-the-shelf wine racking systems, they still may be unsuitable for your cellar or collection's specific needs regardless of their other appealing features. If your space or taste extends beyond commercially available racking, consider a conversion project or a custom-built wine racking system.

Conversions and Custom Racking

There are many kits and instructions available to help you adapt the shelves of a bookcase, entertainment center, or china cabinet for wine storage [see Converting a Bookcase, page 50]. With a few, well-placed stops and scallops to properly support the bottles at their necks and near their bases, almost any shelf or cabinet can be customized for your table wine collection.

You may want to build your own racking from scratch [see Building Wooden racks, page 54]. You may recognize that a custom-designed system is the only way to fit your particular space, capacity, or other special needs. Most custom racking systems utilize several wine storage options, and they may be made of materials that help the system blend into your existing decor.

Custom-built racks allow you to create a unique look for your collection and accommodate irregular spaces in either open-air locations or refrigerated wine cellar spaces. Few commercially available racks, even modular ones, fit the tight angles of an understairs cellar, for instance, or provide for odd-shaped bottles.

Whether you construct a custom racking system yourself or hire a professional to build it to your design, always use high-quality, decay-resistant wood, such as #1, clear-vertical, select-grade redwood or a similar lumber. Besides being stronger and more dimensionally stable than lower-grade materials—important considerations for a conditioned cellar environment—you'll find quality wood easier to work and finish; there will be fewer splits, and the wood accepts paint or stain more evenly than low-grade lumber.

The same rule holds true for other materials. Use only high-gauge, non-corrosive metal (preferably stainless or chrome-coated steel with a powder-coated or rubberized shield to keep it rust-free and help avoid scratching your labels) or ceramic tubes and containers that are clear of cracks, spalls, or chips.

Besides the standard racks, clever pull-out shelving and racking units take advantage of otherwise unusable space and expand the capacity of a cellar.

BUILDING WOODEN RACKS

Vertical wine racks for individual bottle storage are built in modules, called ladders. Each pair of vertical uprights has rungs that will support the bottles. You can change the spacing distance between the rungs and the uprights to hold bottles of different diameters or lengths.

Most wine racks are built with redwood lumber, nominally 1 × 2 for the uprights and 1 × 1 for the rungs. The actual sizes of these two materials are, respectively, ⅝″ × 1½″ (16 × 38 mm) and ⅝″ × ⅝″ (16 × 16 mm), with the 1 × 1s made by ripping 1 × 2 stock down its centerline.

Ladders used for racks that hold standard bottles have uprights that are 12″ (30 cm) apart, with rungs spaced 3¾″ (95 mm) on center. In these standard-bottle racks, the ladders are also spaced 4″ (10 cm) apart, on center. Each pair of ladders 8′ (2.4 m) tall will hold 20 high-shouldered Bordeaux or tapered Burgundy bottles, and they may also hold some bottles of sparkling wine or magnums. Modify the spacing of rungs and ladders to fit bottles of other dimensions such as splits.

Though stiff, ladders are flimsy until you anchor them to a wall and join them with cross-members called rails. All of the rails are laid out on a flat, square work table and marked with their centerline spacings. Next, ladders are placed face down with their bottoms flush, spaced sequentially to the centerline marks, and nailed through the back rail at top and bottom. Finally, the joined rack is turned over and the front rails are nailed to it. It's generally easier to build short modules and join them with continuous front rails than to make one long unit.

Building ladders requires care and precision. You'll need a miter or cutoff saw, a table saw, a wood clamp, squares, and a pneumatic nail gun or hammer, and finish nails.

Materials for One 8′ (2.4 m) Standard Bottle Ladder		
Uprights	**(1)**	1 × 2 × 96″ (16 × 41 × 2,438 mm)
Rungs	**(40)**	1 × 1 (16 × 16 × 305 mm)
Front and Back Rails	**(10)**	1 × 1 (16 × 16 mm)*
*Dimension length to total rack width.		

STEP 1

On a miter or cutoff saw, set an end stop 12″ (30 cm) from the blade and trim groups of rungs to length.

STEP 4

Simultaneously cut two pieces of stock to make spacer blocks 3¾″ (95 mm) long. Square and fasten the first rung, then use the spacers to position each subsequent rung. Turn the ladder in the jig, and fasten rungs on the opposite side.

STEP 2

Set an anti-kickback stop on your table saw with a wood clamp, position the rail fence to equally divide each rung, and test the cut on scrap. When both sides of the rip are equal, rip all of the rung stock. If you want each rung to taper on its front side, set the miter saw to a 15° bevel and make finishing cuts on each piece.

STEP 3

On a flat layout table or other work surface, square and clamp straight pieces of lumber as a jig for master guides. Carefully measure and mark the centerpoint spacing of the ladder's first rung, starting at a point 3¾" (95 mm) above the base edge of the uprights and leaving room for a baseboard molding.

STEP 5

Complete the number of ladders required for your layout. In the cellar, stand ladders on their faces, space them, and fasten back rails to their tops and bottoms. Also attach rails at every sixth row of rungs. Invert and fasten front rails.

STEP 6

Face nail baseboard molding to the rack assembly's foot. To mount the rack to a wall, mark wall studs, stand the rack up, position it, and fasten it with screws through the back rails using a screwdriver with a magnetic, long-handled bit.

Above left: Mount the cellar's air refrigeration system at the highest point in the room. Cool air sinks, and a high mount will keep the temperature constant throughout the space.

Above right: Very narrow areas in understairs cellars are a good choice for horizontal-display shelves. Each shelf needs four inches (10 cm) of depth.

Understairs Wine Cellars

In most homes, the space beneath a stairwell is often finished as a wardrobe or storage closet. Though narrow and irregular, understairs spaces make good wine cellars because they usually are contained within the house structure, or at most share a single outer wall. Convert their interior doors to exterior doors with a tight threshold and weather-stripping to seal the cellar for refrigeration.

A typical staircase is three to four feet (90 to 120 cm) wide. With wine racks a foot (30 cm) wide placed along a sidewall of an understairs closet, it still has two to three feet (60 to 90 cm) of access space. It has ample space beneath the stairs' risers and treads for extra insulation, and it can hold surprisingly large volumes of wine. A typical straight staircase allows sufficient room to hold 400 or more bottles.

It's easy to build a series of successively shorter ladders to fit the slanted ceiling beneath the treads. Under-landing areas also may hold racks, and low-ceiling sections can be outfitted with a combination of vertical or diamond bins or with bulk storage and case shelves.

Mount a split-system refrigeration system with its heat exchanger in the room and its condenser in a remote exterior location, a basement, or the attic. It should be mounted at the highest point in the cellar to assure even temperatures throughout the wine storage area.

Ceramic Racks

Ceramic wine racks, in which the bottles lie in precast tubes, cylinders, clay pipes, or bins, offer a distinctive appearance and feel. They also contribute a small amount of thermal mass to protect the wine from heat, and they reduce the amount of light and vibration the bottles receive. Ceramic racks, however, are massive and less forgiving than wood or metal. Allow for their extra weight and take care when you stock them, as bottles can break more easily and you can scratch their labels against the hard surfaces.

Shelves and Bins

Wood is the most versatile material to use for building custom wine storage systems. With it, you can create shelves, bins, and racks in a variety of shapes, sizes, and designs for a truly unique and accommodating display.

Besides wood racks that suit individual bottles [see Building Wooden Racks, page 54], shelves and bins provide storage and display for cases or multiple bottles of the same type of wine, large or odd-sized bottles, and selections within your collection that deserve special attention. Partly filled bins, however, are less space efficient.

Wooden Display Shelves

Display shelves provide aesthetically pleasing wine storage and give relief from uniform vertical racks. Shelves present individual bottles or, like bookshelves, hold wooden wine cases. Build them into and under counters or sections of vertical racking or create stand-alone shelves in other areas of the cellar.

So-called slant display shelves are flat or slightly tilted. They have a neck support and bottle stops—slightly raised or indented sections of wood —to secure each bottle and prevent it from rolling from side to side. A slight tilt to the shelf allows you to display labels while keeping the bottles' corks submerged and their ullage below the shoulders.

Case storage means either freestanding units secured to a wall or deep recessed shelves built into a wall. Wooden Bordeaux cases are packed with their bottles lying horizontally, and shelves to hold them should accommodate cases set in that position. Case storage is nearly as efficient as individual bottle racking, and it also adds visual interest by showing each winery's insignia branded on its cases.

Shelves can store bulk quantities of bottles as well as wooden cases of wine. Provide a front-edge lip on the shelves to keep bottles from sliding off.

Wooden Bins

Wooden wine storage bins are another way to create visual interest in your cellar or other wine storage location, and they can be easily configured to store multiple and odd-shaped or oversized bottles. Most bins are either rectangular or diamond shaped, and they hold bottles horizontally, stacked directly on top of one another. It is generally best to store one type of wine in a bin, avoiding the necessity of shuffling one wine to access another. Use bins to divide different wines, varietals, or vintages.

This commercial bin display system has a bottle standing up next to the corresponding bin. You'll find such systems in many wine shops and winery tasting rooms. They are intended for short-term storage only; avoid them in a home cellar.

Use caution when you store wine in bins. When bottles are stacked horizontally they can easily slide out of the bin; this is especially true of tapered bottles such as those commonly used for Burgundy or white wines. Bottles in bins also touch one another; use care when you stack them in the bins to avoid breakage.

Rectangular Bins

Rectangular bins typically are four bottles wide and three bottles high, and they hold a full case of loose bottles. They also can be built in a variety of other shapes, sizes, and designs. Most are open—that is, without sides, a solid back, or even a top—allowing the wall behind the racks to contrast with the bottles, but some feature glass-front doors that help keep the bottles free of dust, hold them in place, and permit easy viewing and selection.

Freestanding bins are more akin to furniture or the cabinet islands found in kitchens, and they often include storage drawers, space to hang glassware, and a table- or countertop for opening and decanting wines or for quick tastings. Wine storage, however, remains the priority; configure your bins to accommodate as many bottles as possible, fit otherwise unused spaces in your cellar, and retain easy access to your wine. Consider using double-deep designs that store bottles nose-to-bottom.

Diamond Bins

Diamond bins are a visually appealing option for wine storage. Left backless and open, they allow contrasting wall colors or other features in the room or wine cellar to shine through the open bin, can be structured for use as room dividers, and facilitate airflow through the racking to keep the bottles at proper aging temperature and humidity. As a pure design feature, they also help break up the monotony of a long wall of individual wine bottle racks.

Custom-built diamond bins accommodate the unique and special needs of your wine collection. Built as open boxes, they are fitted with diagonal inserts that securely hold multiple bottles in a horizontal position. Some diamond bins come with half-bin dividers that slide vertically or horizontally into the diamond, dividing it into two sections. Plan to stock each section or the entire bin with the same wine. That way, you can remove the topmost bottles instead of searching the bin for the label you desire.

Build your diamond bins of the same materials and with the same attention to detail as your other racking components for a consistent look. Mix bins and shelves with racks for individual bottles, countertops, archways, and case storage to create visual interest in your wine room. Use bins for long-term storage and aging, then move bottles to individual racks for easier access as the wine matures.

Wooden Individual Bottle Racks

Wine racking systems designed to hold individual bottles are the most common and generally considered the best home for your wine. By far the most modular of all storage options, they can be built to conform to almost any room dimension or configuration. Wooden bottle racks permit air circulation around each bottle, secure the bottles in a stable location free of breakage, and accommodate small or large collections in an efficient, single- or double-

Diamond racking's appealing look conceals its waste of space. Since diamond modules are typically 12 or 16 inches (30 or 40 cm) wide, they hold either 9 or 16 bottles. Neither size fits case-sized lots that contain 12 bottles.

deep, free-standing or wall-mounted system with maximum flexibility.

Most wooden bottle racks are open front and back. They hold each bottle horizontally with side rungs along their entire length. The distance between the vertical uprights are wider than the bottle diameter, while the spaces between the rungs are narrower. Individual bottle racks are often built as a complete rack system that extends vertically and

This slant and individual bottle rack system displays one bottle, and it stores 11 below and 12 above to give a quick two-case inventory to a favorite wine. The display bottle also helps provide visual relief for the racking.

Bottle Shapes and Sizes

Wine bottles come in a variety of shapes and sizes [see page 42]. Though most open-air wine collections and displays feature standard, 750-ml Bordeaux and Burgundy-style bottles, commercial wine racking systems may not accommodate all of their different shapes, much less those of less-standard bottles. Take inventory of your collection and try to anticipate future wine purchases and preferences when you plan your wine racking solution.

horizontally along a wall. Modules are assembled right in the wine cellar, tilted up against the wall, and secured to the room's structure with screws into the framing behind the wallboard, or they are placed freestanding in a back-to-back configuration and anchored to central supports. Fasten multiple racks together before you secure them to the wall.

Measuring about 12 square inches (77 cm²) at their openings, the narrow dimensions of each individual rack assembly allows you to wrap modules around outside and inside corners in pleasing curved configurations; simply install pairs of ladders, taper the side rails, or build them up to maintain the proper width to securely hold each bottle.

Bottle racking systems are commonly one bottle deep and extend 12 to 14 inches (30 to 36 cm) from the wall. Two-bottle-deep configurations, 24 to 28 inches (61 to 71 cm), are ideal for below-counter locations. Use them as you would wall-mounted base kitchen cabinets. Inventory and record your wine collection to identify and find bottles placed behind others in a two-deep racking system.

Planning Racks for Unusual Bottles

Visit any wine shop with a decent inventory and you'll find wine sold in many bottle shapes and sizes [see Common Bottle Shapes and Bottle Sizes charts, at right]. While the so-called full or standard 750-ml (25 oz.) Bordeaux- or Burgundy-style bottles still rule the shelves, even their shapes have changed as wineries increasingly seek to distinguish their labels from one another for marketing purposes and competitive advantage. Tapered, ultra-thin, and square-based bottles, along with those that hold 1.5 liters (50 oz.) and 3.0 liters (100 oz.)—or even more— have become more common in recent years. There are even production wines sold in plastic bladders packed into cardboard boxes.

Bottles in unique shapes and sizes are the exceptions to the rules of design that wreak havoc on racking systems. While custom-built shelves or racks or bins can accommodate larger-volume bottles, odd-sized bottles present the greatest challenge— especially for off-the-shelf racking systems and individual bottle racks designed primarily to store standard bottles. These bottles are difficult to store in positions that will keep their corks moist, yet in conditions that are stable and secure.

Examine recent additions to your wine collection and try to anticipate future needs as you plan a wine racking solution for your cellar. If your collection contains many bottles in unusual shapes or sizes, consider devoting part of the space to bins or shelves instead of individual bottle racks, and use them to store and display your unusual bottles.

Finally, remember that of all the features of your wine cellar, racking is the most adaptable to future change. Should you discover that some bins or shelves are gathering dust, reconfigure your storage.

Common Bottle Shapes (750 ml/25 oz.)

Bottle Type	Length		Diameter
Bordeaux	11.5″ (292 mm)	×	3″ (75 mm)
Burgundy	11.5″ (292 mm)	×	3.25″ (83 mm)
Rhine	14″ (356 mm)	×	2.75″ (70 mm)
Chianti fiasco	10.5″ (267 mm)	×	4″ (102 mm)
Bocksbeutel	8.5″ (216 mm)	×	6″ (152 mm)
Port or Sherry*	11.5″ (292 mm)	×	3.5″ (89 mm)
Champagne/ sparkling wine	12.5″ (318 mm)	×	3.25″ (83 mm)

*Sizes vary considerably.

Bottle Sizes†

Bottle	Volume	Dimensions (Length × Diameter)
Quarter Bottle	187 ml (6 oz.)	7″ × 2″ (178 × 50 mm)
Half Bottle/Split	375 ml (13 oz.)	9.5″ × 2.25″ (241 × 57 mm)
Full or Standard Bottle	750 ml (25 oz.)	11.5″ × 3″ (292 × 75 mm)
Magnum	1.5 liters (50 oz.)	13.5″ × 4″ (343 × 102 mm)
Jeroboam*	3 liters (100 oz.)	18″ × 5″ (457 × 127 mm)
Methuselah*	6 liters (200 oz.)	22.25″ × 6″ (565 × 152 mm)
Salmanazar*	9 liters (300 oz.)	27.5″ × 7″ (699 × 178 mm)
Balthazar*	12 liters (400 oz.)	29″ × 8″ (737 × 203 mm)
Nabuchadnezzar*	16 liters (540 oz.)	34″ × 9″ (864 × 228 mm)

*Referred to as Indian or biblical names in the wine trade.

† Sizes may vary.

INSTALLING SELF-CONTAINED WINE APPLIANCES

Wine appliances are easy to install and convenient to use.

Prefabricated, self-contained wine storage units bridge the gap between unconditioned wine storage and custom-designed-and-built, refrigerated wine cellars. As with any wine storage solution, review your needs, those of your collection, and the space available in your home before you choose a wine appliance.

Stand-alone wine appliances feature built-in mechanical systems and racks. They are as easy to install as other electrical components and are ready to use as soon as you plug them in.

Place wine appliances in the areas of your home where you entertain, relax, and prepare food, either as your sole cellar or as an auxiliary storage area.

By contrast, built-in wine storage units are installed under counters, along walls, or set within enclosures such as a closet. They require site preparation and some demolition, utility connections and extensions—possibly added vents—and you must apply finishes before you can use them. Construction makes built-ins somewhat more complex to install than stand-alone units but definitely easier than installing a complete custom wine room.

Wine storage appliances offer more precise aging than simple shelving, and you can rotate your wine collection as you would in a custom-built cellar.

AN OVERVIEW

Whether you choose a built-in wine appliance or a stand-alone unit that features the look of fine furniture, opt for one with the necessary features to protect your wine.

Self-contained wine storage appliances provide temperature and humidity control in off-the-shelf units. Those most commonly seen are similar in size to small-capacity refrigerators, but there are also large-capacity models that hold 750 bottles or more. They feature climate controls, humidity-recovery systems, insulated and airtight walls and doors, and racking appropriate for wine storage and aging.

Built-in under-counter wine appliances are a convenient answer for storing small amounts of wine in kitchens, dining rooms, or other serving areas.

A self-contained unit is either freestanding or built into cabinetry and walls in the same manner used for kitchen appliances such as dishwashers and trash compactors. The large-capacity units stand in cabinetry bays or are built into alcoves. Options exist to outfit them with a variety of different door fronts and cabinetry surrounds that match your existing decor. Most also have tinted and insulated glass fronts to display the wines they contain. Both types of unit require electrical outlets; they may need dedicated circuits, depending on capacity.

The primary benefits of such appliances are their convenience and economy. With furniture-like detailing, freestanding units can be placed almost anywhere serviced by a standard 110-volt electrical outlet [see Utility Requirements for Installation, pg. 66]. Built-ins, while requiring a bit of carpentry, are easier and quicker to install than cellars built from scratch.

Popular self-contained wine storage units provide capacity to store small to medium-sized collections. They can supplement a larger cellar located in a basement, garage, or outbuilding, chill wine for a party or tasting, and house wines that have different temperature and humidity levels than are possible in a larger storage area.

Capacity and reliance on fixed shelving are two drawbacks worth mentioning. Wine appliances will usually hold only 750 ml Bordeaux bottles and some Burgundy bottles. A large-capacity unit, especially one designed and finished as furniture, may actually cost more than a custom cellar. In most cases, it will still lack a flexible, custom racking system.

Use the following decision points to help decide if a prefabricated, self-contained wine storage unit is right for you:

- Will you have a limited-capacity collection (30 to 750 bottles)?
- Will it consist primarily or exclusively of standard-sized and shaped (750-ml) bottles?
- Do you have a location with convenient access to a 110-volt electrical outlet?
- Are you willing to sacrifice under-counter cabinet space, a wall area, or closet space for a wine appliance?
- Do you need supplemental wine storage beyond your main cellar?
- Do you rent an apartment or are you subject to frequent moves that make a permanent wine cellar project impossible?
- Are other areas of your home unsuitable for conditioned wine storage?

Standard racks included in both wine appliances and refrigerated furniture units can be inadequate for storing large or unusually shaped bottles.

Remember, the designs of some wine appliances make them undesirable for long-term storage of fine wines, so review all of their features before you choose a unit. Avoid those with excess noise, vibration, or too-dry conditions inside the appliance. Remember that, in some locations, glass doors may allow too much light to reach the wine. Finally, should the unit's mechanical system fail, will you be able to relocate the wine inside it until the appliance is repaired?

CHOOSING A LOCATION

Whether you choose an under-counter site, placement within a furniture piece, or install an appliance as a free-standing unit, meet ideal site requirements for best performance.

Spots adjacent to sinks, islands, or ranges often contain electrical outlets used for dishwashers, trash compactors, or counter appliances. These locations are easy installation-areas for a wine chiller built into cabinetry.

Many of the same rules of thumb apply when you select a location for a self-contained wine storage appliance as for placing an ambient-temperature wine rack in a room or cabinet. By contrast, wine appliances require electricity and access to ventilation, which often dictate their location in a room.

With the range of choices available for freestanding and built-in units, the size of the appliance—and the space it will require in a room—depends as much on your wine collection as on its location. Choose an appliance with capacity to hold the necessary number of bottles, match it to the scale of your room's other furnishings, and select a spot with convenient access to the unit.

Freestanding units are the most flexible regarding space requirements and placement, and they can be moved to new locations. Built-in units, on the other hand, require careful space planning; they occupy permanent places in your rooms, frequently converted from another use.

In kitchens or bars, install wine appliances under the counters in existing runs of base cabinets [see Installing a Wine Chiller, page 68]. You'll need to choose a

Utility Requirements for Installation

A freestanding, self-contained wine storage appliance with a capacity of less than 100 bottles simply plugs into a standard, 110-volt electrical outlet, optimally on a dedicated circuit. Larger units with correspondingly greater capacity and refrigeration loads may require a 220-volt circuit, the same service needed for a full-size refrigerator-freezer. While most built-in units have front or top venting, take care to provide adequate ventilation for the appliance as specified by the manufacturer, and allow ample clearance on the top, sides, and back of the unit to increase airflow.

site with accessible electricity, possibly by removing and replacing a trash compactor or dishwasher. Depending on the unit's requirements and your home's construction, you can extend an existing electrical run to the appliance through the walls or under the floor. Most 110-volt outlets in kitchens are adjacent to sinks, ranges, refrigerators, and ovens. They are easy to extend; run wiring from the existing outlet above the countertop through the interior of the wall and into the back of the appliance cabinet. You can also wire new circuits from the service panel to the appliance through the basement or crawl space below, or above through the ceiling joists.

Overlay maple facings blend in a large, built-in wine appliance to other kitchen cabinetry. Such overlays are custom-made to the needs of the specific unit and installed after the unit is in place.

For either appliance type, choose locations near glass and food storage, flatware, and utensils. The elements you'll need for a tasting party or meal will be within easy reach.

Besides choosing a site with ample space for the unit, customize your wine appliance to your room's existing decor. While most wine units are sold with tinted glass doors that have the dual purpose of displaying the bottles and protecting the wine, consider custom door fronts, facings, and enclosures that match or contrast with the style of cabinets already in the room. Many manufacturers offer overlay cabinet fronts for wine appliances that complement standard kitchen cabinets or provide for custom facings. Wine appliances also come in stainless steel and colored enamel finishes that harmonize with other appliances. Freestanding units are offered in wood or tasteful metal finishes.

INSTALLING A WINE CHILLER

Installing a wine chiller appliance in an existing trash compactor or dishwasher bay is simplicity itself: you carefully remove the old appliance, unplug it, and slide the new unit into its place. It is also easy to lift many kitchen counters, slide out an existing base cabinet, and insert a wine appliance. Repurposing an existing cabinet, however, requires careful attention to finish carpentry.

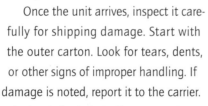

Preparation is the key to a good installation. Evaluate locations in your kitchen, butler pantry, dining room, or other location before choosing the unit. Note its dimensions—height, width, and depth—along with any clearance requirements necessary for installation. Choose only appliances specifically designed as built-ins; you'll recognize them by their front or top vents, which allow room air to enter and exhaust from the refrigeration system.

Once the unit arrives, inspect it carefully for shipping damage. Start with the outer carton. Look for tears, dents, or other signs of improper handling. If damage is noted, report it to the carrier. Next, open the carton and check that all components are free of damage and all supplied parts are present. Plug in the unit and test its operation. Only when you are satisfied that the unit is in good condition should you proceed to install it.

The installation process shown here depicts all the steps you'll need to take to remove one bay of a base cabinet without disturbing its countertop or the adjacent cabinets.

To begin, you'll need a tape measure, wrenches, screwdrivers, carpentry tools, and materials to match your cabinet walls, facings, and moldings. Carefully follow the steps shown to remove the old cabinet facing and prepare the opening to receive the wine appliance.

Allow about four hours to complete the demolition and reconstruction phases of a base cabinet before you can install the wine appliance.

STEP 1

As a final check before beginning installation, measure the outer dimensions of the unit to confirm that ample space exists in your site for it to clear top, bottom, back, and sides. There should be an all-around minimum clearance of ½" (12 mm)—more if the appliance's manufacturer requires additional clearance space.

STEP 4

With a screwdriver, remove the screws holding the center stile from the rail and tap the stile from its position with a mallet. If it is nailed and glued, cut the stile flush at the rail with a box saw before removing it.

STEP 2

When you are satisfied that the appliance will fit the space, remove drawers and cabinet doors. Many flush-mounted Euro-style hinge sets have release clamps that grip the hinge mechanism. Press down on the clip to free the door from its hinge. For traditional cabinet hinges, remove the screws that fasten the hinge to the door.

STEP 3

Remove all hinge and drawer hardware. A cordless electric screwdriver or a drill mounted with a screwdriver bit makes short work of hardware removal. Place hinge sets, screws, and hardware in a sealable plastic bag, and mark it for other use. Slide a hacksaw blade between the shelf and sidewall, cutting nails along its width. Tap out the shelf.

STEP 5

To narrow the side and center stiles, mark the centerpoint of the stiles and carefully make horizontal cuts to the marks with a box saw. Make each cut perpendicular to the surface by aligning the saw's face with the cabinet sidewall.

STEP 6

Use a carpenter's square to mark straight lines down the center of each stile. After the lines are marked, check the total width of the future opening compared to the wine appliance's width clearance requirements.

MAKING AN APPLIANCE OPENING

With the drawers, doors, hardware, dividing stile, and center shelf removed, the next step is to enlarge the cabinet's opening for the new wine appliance. The opening for the new wine appliance will fill the area occupied by half of an old double base cabinet. Convert the space by narrowing the stiles to half of their original width, cutting the side stile flush with the sidewall.

Careful carpentry is required to achieve a good result. As a general rule, hand tools permit greater control than a power reciprocating or jigsaw. Use a box saw with fine teeth when making stile cuts, take your time, and keep the cut straight along its entire length. When you are finished, these cuts will show along the face of the cabinet adjacent to the wine chiller.

Besides cuts made to the cabinet face members, the cabinet bottom shelf and support will also be removed to make space occupied by the wine appliance. Use a power jigsaw for these cuts, drilling a starting hole with one edge of the hole aligned to the cut line. Finish the cut with a handsaw at the back edge of the shelf. The cut made at the sidewall must be done with a handsaw.

With the cabinet bottom removed, make vertical cuts down the sidewall through the toekick, face veneer, and molding to open the area for the appliance. Finally, check the vertical clearance, mark and cut away the top rail under the countertop.

Next, you will reconstruct the sidewalls and shelves of the other half of the cabinet.

STEP 7

Cut vertically up the stile centerline, removing pieces as they become free. Work slowly and carefully, keeping the blade vertical as you make the cut. Bracing the cut members with your hands or a carpentry clamp will help keep the saw from binding.

STEP 10

Remove the cut base shelf. Cut the toekick plate, veneer, and molding until the cut is level to the floor. Repeat at the old center stile's centerline, rather than lining up with the cut made for the bottom shelf.

STEP 8

Cut down the centerline of the right lower side stile, keeping the saw blade parallel to the cabinet sidewall. Minor cut marks on the sidewall will be hidden in the finished installation, but the cuts in the cabinet face should be smooth and straight.

STEP 9

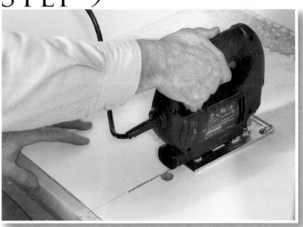

Mark a line perpendicular to the cabinet face, set back ¾" (19 mm) from the old front stile centerline toward the cabinet that will remain. The allowance will be used when you install a new left sidewall. Drill a pilot hole in the base shelf and cut it with a jigsaw. Depending on the appliance's and cabinet's depth, your cut may stop short of the backwall.

STEP 11

Measure the height of the unit, allow ½" (12 mm) more height, and mark the cut on the top rail of the cabinet. Drill a pilot hole aligned with the line and cut free the rail. The opening should now fit the wine appliance dimensions.

STEP 12

Sand all cut faces with a vibrating sander and 100-grit sandpaper until the saw marks are gone. Change to 200-grit sandpaper, and finish the edges of the stiles and rails. Touch up with an appropriate stain, paint, or varnish.

RESTORATION AND INSTALLATION

Now that the cabinet opening has been cut to receive the new wine appliance, the next steps in the installation process restore the left side of the cabinet to usability. First, you must fit a new side panel in the space behind the cabinet face, fasten it to the cut base shelf and top with nails or screws, and then reattach the face stile—once you have cut it lengthwise to half its original width. Later, a new middle shelf will be installed and the drawer hardware will be reattached to the stile.

When the cabinet restoration is completely finished, an access port is cut in the sidewall of the new appliance bay, granting a path for an electrical cord to an existing dishwasher and disposal outlet beneath the adjacent kitchen sink cabinet.

The appliance being installed is rated at two amps with a peak load at start-up of less than four amps. The existing 20-amp disposal circuit has ample capacity for the new appliance. The dishwasher is on its own dedicated circuit, and there are open outlets on the circuit powering the waste disposal. This situation is typical for a newly constructed house built to code.

If a new circuit had been required, it would have been routed by an electrician from the main service panel, through the wall's stud cavities, and into the appliance bay. A new circuit breaker would have been installed with the appropriate amperage rating for an appliance run.

When the wine appliance unit's power cord has been fed through the port and plugged in, the unit is ready to slide back into the new bay in the cabinet.

These wine appliance installation steps will take about two hours to complete.

STEP 13

Cut cabinet stock to fit the opening from the floor to the counter—here, melamine-faced particle board was used throughout the existing cabinetry. This side panel should fit into the recess left when the original bottom shelf was cut, tucking behind the stile and toekicks.

STEP 16

When the rail's glue is set, use an electric drill fitted with a spade bit to drill partway through the sidewall of the cabinet 4" (10 cm) above the old bottom shelf location. Stop when the pilot tip of the bit emerges from the sidewall in the next cabinet. Complete the port from the other side.

STEP 14

Fasten the new side panel to the bottom shelf with a pneumatic nail gun with wire brads or a hammer with finish nails. Carefully mark the location of the shelf on the nailing side and level the nail gun to ensure that the fasteners hit the center of the shelf.

STEP 15

Rip the old stile in half on a table or band saw. Apply woodworker's glue to the face of the new side panel and the ends of the rail. Position the rail with its edge in line with its prior location, and clamp it in place with wood clamps. Allow the glue to dry completely before proceeding.

STEP 17

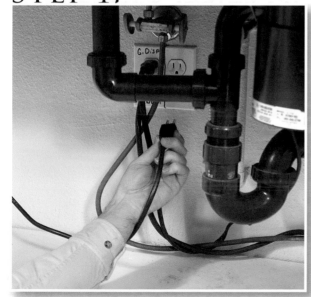

Move the wine appliance to a spot near its bay, feed its power cord through the access port, and plug it into the electrical outlet. Always turn off the power to the circuit at the main panel before connecting a kitchen appliance to an electrical outlet, then restore the power.

STEP 18

Slide the wine appliance back into its bay, keeping it square with the sidewalls and level with the floor. The unit's front face—the frame to which its door hinges are attached—either should be flush with the cabinet face or protrude about ¼" (6 mm), depending on the model.

FINISHING THE INSTALLATION

STEP 19

The new wine appliance next must be raised to touch the top rail and leveled by adjusting its feet. The adjacent cabinet's drawer and hinge hardware are reattached. If desired, a new center shelf can be added by drilling mounting holes in the sidewalls, inserting shelf hangers, and cutting a shelf to fit the space.

When the installation is complete, test the unit's operation, allowing it to run for several hours. Use a household thermometer to fine-tune the temperature settings if the unit lacks a digital readout. It should settle and hold a single temperature within a degree once its interior walls and the racks have cooled. Check the operation of the fans, and be sure that the internal drip pan at the base is correctly positioned.

Your unit is ready to stock with wine. For vintages that will be held for some time before drinking, load the unit and lower the wine's temperatures gradually over a period of hours rather than quickly cooling it. Sudden lowering temperatures cause the wine to contract, drawing air through the bottle cork. These precautions are unnecessary for white, sparkling, and red table wines.

Monitor the unit for the first several weeks of its operation. If it should fail or have unsteady performance, contact the manufacturer to repair or replace the unit. A properly installed wine appliance is usually reliable for many years.

The procedures for installing other under-counter wine appliances are basically the same as those demonstrated here. Always read completely and follow exactly the manufacturer's installation procedures for your specific model, as failure to do so may void the unit's warranty.

Remember that kitchen cabinets frequently are in close proximity to pressurized water supply and wastewater pipes as well as gas and electrical lines. When working, always exercise caution to avoid personal hazard or injury, and wear protective eyewear and gloves when you operate power saws and other tools.

Allow about an hour to finish the project.

All refrigeration systems must be level in order to operate properly. They contain liquid coolant that is progressively compressed and then evaporated to collect and disburse heat; for the liquid to flow through the coils of the heat exchanger, the unit must be level. Check both sides with a carpenter's square, and use a hand level to check front to back level. Adjust the turnscrews on the unit's feet to move each of the four corners up and down. For best appearance, the top of the cabinet should be nearly flush with the top cabinet rail.

STEP 20

Reattach the doors to the adjacent cabinet. A new middle shelf for the remaining cabinet can be installed with shelf-mounting clips in drilled holes, or you can leave the door off and mount wineglass hanging hardware in it.

STEP 21

Turn the unit on and set its temperature control. Check that appliance lights operate properly. Use a household thermometer or the digital readout on the unit to monitor the cooling function and any temperature variation.

STEP 22

When you are satisfied that the wine chiller is operating properly, set it to the desired temperature for the type of wine it will hold and fill the racks with bottles. Fill out and mail the manufacturer's warranty card. It may take 24 hours or more for the wine to reach its final temperature, and during this time the unit may run more frequently than will be the case once it contains a large volume of wine at a common temperature. Good appliances will keep the temperature inside them constant to within one or two degrees.

WINE APPLIANCE IN A CLOSET

A seldom-used wardrobe or linen closet makes a great spot for installing a built-in full-sized wine appliance. Most standard closets are three to four feet (90 to 120 cm) wide and two feet (60 cm) deep, with a centered door opening that is 30 to 34 inches (76 to 86 cm) wide. Wine appliance manufacturers make models designed to fit in such spaces that usually hold 120 to 160 bottles of wine.

Stand-alone appliances and those made with special clips to allow attaching custom cabinet overlays are a good choice for a closet retrofit. Some suppliers have both unit types in their lines, so ask for expert advice when deciding on the appliance you want.

The first steps in the installation process are to remove the old door, its frame, and the shelving of the closet.

To begin, you'll need a tape measure, wrenches, screwdrivers, carpentry tools, and materials to match your household's cabinets, facings, and floor moldings. Carefully follow the steps shown to renovate the closet to receive the wine appliance.

Allow about an hour to remove the closet's interior elements, its door, and the doorjamb.

STEP 1

Remove the door hinge pins, beginning with the center hinge. Tap the top hinge partially out. Support the door, then remove its bottom and top pins.

STEP 4

Use a utility knife to score the paint at the junction between the jamb strip and the frame. Repeat at the junction of the casing molding and the threshold.

STEP 2

Remove the door from the closet. Store it away from the work area. Keep it for use in another project or discard it.

STEP 3

Remove the door hinges from the door frame with an electric screwdriver or power drill mounted with a screwdriver bit.

STEP 5

Insert the chisel teeth of a pry bar into the space between the jamb molding and the frame. Working along its length, remove the molding. Keep or discard it.

STEP 6

Using the same method, pry the door casing molding from the face and back of the threshold. Keep it for use in repairs of your house or discard it.

DEMOLITION AND WIRING

Complete the demolition of the closet. After the casing moldings have been removed, use a rubber mallet to remove linen shelves and a pry bar to lift the support rails. For closets fitted with shelf-support hardware, remove the shelves, then use a screwdriver to take off the support rails and clips. All of the interior surfaces of the closet will be hidden when you complete the project.

The final step is removing the door casing. Casings are usually shimmed in place and fastened with stout nails to make them strong. The rough door opening may be out of alignment when the casing is removed, and instructions are given later in the process for correcting it or changing the height or width of the door opening to accommodate your wine appliance's dimensions.

Once the closet has been removed, the next step is to wire a new dedicated circuit to the site. Full-size wine appliances usually require either a dedicated 15-amp or 20-amp circuit, depending on the model. They draw as much power on start-up as a household refrigerator. Always consult the manufacturer's specifications when planning electrical runs, use a licensed tradesman, and obtain necessary municipal approvals for electrical modifications to your home.

Schedule time with an electrician so that all of the work is completed before your wine appliance is planned for delivery. Depending on the length of the run, allow about two hours to complete the electrical work and two hours to enlarge the opening.

STEP 7

With a rubber mallet, tap sharply upward on each shelf to free it from the support rail. Shelves may be glued or nailed, and considerable effort may be necessary to remove them.

STEP 10

Turn off all power to the house. At the main electrical panel of the house, add a new circuit breaker rated for the amperage required. Label the circuit.

STEP 8

Insert the pry bar into the door casing. Work the bar up and down to pull the casing nails from the studs. Avoid prying on the adjacent wallboard, which will be retained.

STEP 9

A door casing is usually destroyed as it is removed. Pull out the casing, and discard it. Pull all remaining nails, staples, and brads, leaving a clean surface.

STEP 11

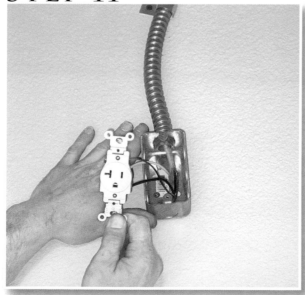

Run cable of the proper amperage and rating from the panel to the closet. Use conduit for surface runs. Attach an appliance-rated outlet, and test the polarity and ground.

STEP 12

If necessary, remove the existing trimmer studs and the header. Cut back the wallboard or plaster to fit the new opening.

PREPARING AND INSTALLING

With the old header and trimmer studs removed, check the dimensions of your wine appliance. You may have to increase the height or width of the opening, or both may need to be adjusted in order to accommodate the unit.

Most closets are built in leftover spaces and have headers designed solely to hold wallboard. They are not structural elements, but you should always use caution and additional bracing inside the closet whenever you remove headers from a doorway. A 2 × 4 that spans the opening, mounts flush against the ceiling, and has a supporting upright in each corner of the closet is usually sufficient bracing for rebuilding a closet header.

The existing header spans the opening between two king studs that run from the floor sill to the top plate. The header is further supported by a trimmer stud beneath it and a cripple stud above it. To widen the opening, remove the trimmer studs and, if necessary, the king studs, mounting replacements spaced the correct distance for your wine appliance. Level and square all construction before nailing.

When the opening has been enlarged, unpack and inspect the wine appliance for shipping damage. Consult the installation directions and check all dimensions and the location of electrical components before proceeding.

Enlist the aid of helpers to move the wine appliance to the closet site, using a special refrigerator hand truck with support feet—they are available for hourly rental at equipment suppliers. Full-sized wine appliances may weigh 500 pounds (227 kg) or more. The retailer that supplied the unit may suggest installers or other laborers familiar with moving large and awkward wine appliances.

STEP 1

Measure, mark, and trim the cripple studs with a reciprocating saw, allowing 1½″ (38 mm) for the new header. Always exercise extreme caution and wear protective eyewear when working overhead with such saws due to their hazardous nature and potential for injury.

STEP 4

Open the unit packing, using care to avoid scratching the face components. Leave all shipping screws, tape, and protective wrap in place until the unit is at the installation location and is ready for mounting.

STEP 2

Cut a 2 × 4 to length, shim it level, and nail it to the cripple studs. Toenail it to the king studs or drill pilot holes and fasten it to the king studs with deck screws.

STEP 3

Cut new 2 × 4 trimmer studs to length, square them with a carpenter's framing level, check the width of the opening, and if necessary shim between the king and trimmer studs. Nail them to the king studs.

STEP 5

Remove all of the shelves before moving the wine appliance and exercise caution—appliances are heavy and prone to toppling. Always use helpers and proper equipment made for the job when transporting heavy appliances.

STEP 6

Install an antitip bar to the back wall of the closet. It should extend at least 3½" (89 mm) over the unit and be ¼" (6 mm) above the unit's top. It will prevent the unit from tipping forward as the door opens and the pull-out shelves extend.

FINISHING THE INSTALLATION

Installing a full-sized wine appliance in a prepared opening is easy work other than moving the unit itself. Many appliances are mounted on nylon-coated feet to help them slide, and these feet are adjustable from the front of the unit once it is in place in the opening.

Always plug the unit in prior to installation and check the function of its refrigeration, humidity, lighting, and controls. When you are satisfied that the unit is operating properly, turn it off and then turn off the circuit by tripping the breaker at the main electrical panel.

The wine appliance should be positioned in the opening as directed by the manufacturer. Self-contained units have all of the necessary framing and trims to complete their installation. Here, a custom cabinet enclosure will be installed to show how a built-in appliance can blend with other kitchen cabinetry.

Overlay cabinetry is usually supplied by a cabinet specialist. It must be made to precise dimensions to allow it to be installed on the unit. Some units have separate panels to retain the cabinetry and faceplates that attach to them. Others are single-piece units. Most complicated are frames that surround an insulated glass door.

Obtain the specifications for a cabinetry overlay at the time you order your appliance and arrange for a cabinet maker to construct the overlay. Allow as long as four to six weeks for delivery of the components, and schedule the installation of the appliance after the overlay cabinet components are delivered.

Allow a half hour to test, install, and level the unit and another hour to install the cabinet overlay.

STEP 1

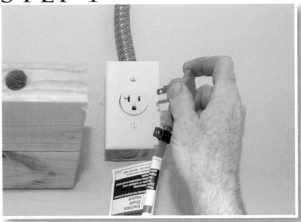

With the unit at the opening, plug the appliance into the electrical outlet. Check that the power cord moves freely from the top of the unit and is not caught between the appliance and the antitip bar.

STEP 4

Use an open-end or socket wrench to adjust the front feet, checking the unit with a carpenter's level. Adjust the back feet with the front-adjusting screws until the unit is level.

STEP 2

Turn the unit on and check its operation. Set the temperature and humidity level (if it is a feature), and turn the unit's lighting system on and off. When you are satisfied that the unit is operating correctly, turn it off and cut the power to the circuit at the main panel.

STEP 3

With a helper, move the unit back into the prepared closet opening. Keep its face parallel to the wall, and slide the unit straight back. It should rest under the antitip bar with its face, to which the door is attached, flush with the wallboard on each side of the opening.

STEP 5

Mount the cabinet door overlay following the manufacturer's directions. Most slide into guides or clips, then are fastened with screws through the door frame.

STEP 6

Surround the unit with an outer cabinet frame mounted flush with the unit's face. Metal elements of the appliance are barely visible with the wood overlay in place.

USING SELF-CONTAINED WINE STORAGE UNITS

When it's time to fill your wine appliance for the first time, follow these tips to give your collection an easy transition.

After installing your self-contained wine storage unit, stock it with wine according to your tastes and needs. If the unit has a separate humidifier tray, fill it with water or place a damp sponge in it. Add a few drops of household bleach—sodium hypochlorite—to the water at each refilling to keep the unit's humidifier free of mold.

If the wine appliance has an adjustable racking system, adjust it to suit the sizes and shapes of the bottles that you collect and organize the wine by label and grape varietal—as well as by the relative age of each bottle in your collection.

For a small-capacity, under-the-counter unit, arrange the wine so that the bottles you will use first or the groups you drink most often will be near the top and front of the wine appliance. Place younger vintages and reserve wines deeper in the appliance, giving them time to age without disturbing them as you extract other bottles.

Also, organize the wine to allow proper rotation and replenishment. Gauge your consumption and purchasing habits so that well-aged wine is always at the ready, with a cache of some younger vintages still in the process of reaching their peak. If the unit's

Fine furniture for wine? A self-contained cellar can be equipped with custom racks and dual refrigeration systems suited to the most careful cellar master's taste, yet still retain its beauty and be a tasteful reminder of your passion for the grape.

capacity permits, plan to include a few bottles of nonvintage or production table wine to drink with family meals.

Quality self-contained units are designed to provide the proper temperature and humidity for aging and storing wine. They only differ from a full climate-controlled cellar in the number of bottles they hold and possibly their ability to maintain relative humidity levels in the proper range. Many are capable of both temperature and humidity controls equivalent to a regular wine cellar.

Opposite page: For first stocking, fill the unit with wine, then slowly bring the temperature down to your desired setting.

Custom racking within a wine furniture piece accommodates magnums and other large bottles such as those used for sparkling wines. Cool-burning LED rope lights improves label readability while the door is open, then turn off when it closes.

Calculate how long a particular label or vintage needs to age using the same methods as you would for other climate-controlled wine storage [see Wine Aging Recommendations, page 159]. Assume that you will maintain a constant temperature inside the appliance and limit the wine's exposure to heat, light, and excessive vibration.

Keep an eye on your self-contained wine appliance's capacity and avoid purchasing more wine than the unit can accommodate. Use several units situated in entertainment, kitchen, or dining areas of your home, giving you more space to age and store a growing wine collection while maintaining flexibility.

Initial Recommendations for Use

When you first install your wine appliance, check its temperature regularly to assure yourself that variation is limited. After a few days, set the temperature to the lower range of room temperature—65°F (18°C)—and stock the unit with wine. Give it several days at that temperature before beginning to lower it. Over a week or more, bring the temperature down to the desired level for aging your collection. This gradual adaptation will limit bottle shock and prevent fresh air entering the bottles through their corks.

Such adaptation is only required for the first stocking of the unit. Feel free to acquire and add bottles to your collection as others are used. The shock of entering your appliance will be minimal compared to the temperature variations they likely experienced en route to your wine shop from the winery.

Make it a habit to periodically check the proper operation of the unit—about once every two weeks is right. Note how often the unit cycles on and off, and whether the fans are operating. Should you experience a mechanical breakdown, keep the wine in the unit until the repair person can service the unit. Wine appliances are heavily insulated and, when fully stocked with wine, have ample thermal mass to keep temperature variations minimal for periods up to 36 hours providing you keep the door closed.

If a longer service interruption is expected, or if the unit must be removed and taken away for repair, plan to store your collection in the coolest, most stable area of your home. Remember, it's the wine's future you're protecting.

Larger wine appliances can hold wood Bordeaux boxes on their lower shelves, an excellent way to display a great vintage as well as age the wine.

CHAPTER 5

PLANNING AND BUILDING A WINE CELLAR

Build a wine cellar following step-by-step directions.

Consider a custom wine cellar if your hobby has grown into a fascination with all things wine and you have both the resources and a suitable space for it in your home. An in-home cellar will serve the specific needs of your collection, reflect your love of wine, and increase your home's value. Building a cellar is more complicated than converting shelving, mounting racks, or installing wine appliances—it's an endeavor similar in scope, budget, and schedule to a kitchen or bath remodel. A wine cellar requires refrigeration, structural supports for racks and equipment, insulation, thermal mass, and moisture control to create a room suitable for finishing with your choice of racks, counters, and light fixtures.

Before you prepare to build a wine room, you will gain a general understanding of your home's construction and all of the features unique to wine cellars.

Begin with a basic understanding of your home. It'll help you decide whether to tackle the job yourself or hire a contractor to do some or all of your cellar's construction; either way, a general background is useful. Stay in your comfort zone and skill level as you define your role. It's generally best to use professionals for electrical work, refrigeration systems, and plumbing.

GENERAL CONSIDERATIONS, PLANNING, AND PREPARATION

As you choose a space for your wine cellar, give ample thought to all of its requirements and the features that you desire.

Proposals made by a wine cellar contractor should include examples of prior work and references from former clients, detailed plans for the project, and a budget for materials and labor.

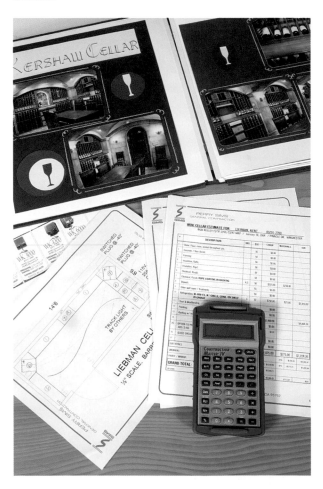

Building a custom wine room requires an overall understanding of design and construction terms, techniques, options, and materials, and how these elements work together to create an ideal wine storage environment. Your wine room will be a permanent structure; while you may be able to adjust or remodel the racking systems to accommodate a growing collection, think of the room and its systems as permanent parts of your home.

Therefore, look for a location that balances capacity and convenience, employs an unused space (or one for which its previous use can be easily relocated or sacrificed), and provides reasonable access for extension of circuits and plumbing to new mechanical systems. Ideally, the cellar should use existing structural components of the house for some or all of the walls, the floor, and the ceiling.

If you're considering a below-grade location, for instance, choose an accessible corner where you can use the existing basement walls for two of the cellar's walls—you'll cut the expense of building them from scratch. Another good location is an interior space wholly within the home's exterior walls. Interior spaces have nearly constant, comfortable temperatures higher than those of the planned wine storage area, and they are isolated from the temperature swings typical of exterior walls. Be practical; if you choose a closet or understairs location, find somewhere else to store coats, boots, holiday decorations, and board games.

The project's budget is another critical consideration. Your resources for the project drive the design process, so settle them first. This assures that you will gain reasonable estimate for the cost of the project.

While locations such as basements are suited for so-called passive cooling, in which the surroundings regulate the climate without the aid of mechanical systems, they are generally unreliable for supplying the consistent climate control needed for a wine cellar environment [see Passive Cooling, page 93]. More often, plan to install active refrigeration and humidity-control systems, regardless of your wine room's location. They will create and maintain ideal conditions for proper storage and aging of wine.

Several key factors determine which is the right refrigeration system for your cellar, including room volume, location, and the construction of the walls, floor, and ceiling.

Cooling systems are designed and sized according to the volume of the area they cool, the desired temperature conditions for the space, and the combined structure and features of the finished space, such as its insulation, moisture protection, and seals and weather-stripping components.

Proper insulation slows the natural warming and cooling of the wine cellar. Consult a heating, ventilation, and air-conditioning (HVAC) contractor or engineering professional who can calculate how well the insulated walls, door, and windows—if any— will slow temperature changes in the cellar and make specific insulation recommendations.

Typical wine cellars have interior walls and floors insulated to at least R-13 and its exterior walls and ceilings to R-19—or to R-30 if a wall is exposed to strong winds or direct sunlight or the ceiling divides the cellar from nonconditioned space. The quality of the room's insulation determines the demand or

An insulated door with tight weather-stripping seals and a threshold sweep helps keep cool, moist air in the wine cellar. This wine room also has walls and ceilings with heavy insulation, and a natural-stone floor that provides passive thermal mass to aid the room's refrigeration system.

load on the cooling system necessary to maintain the cellar's climate, which in turn dictates the capacity and specific model chosen for the refrigeration system. The better the insulation and seals, the smaller and more energy-efficient is the cooling equipment required. A bit less accurate gauge is to size your cooling equipment using the cubic footage of the space or the number of bottles of wine the room holds.

Most self-contained refrigeration systems can cool the air in the room only 30°F (17°C) below the ambient temperature outside the enclosure. If the outdoor temperatures in your climate exceed 85°F (29°C)— and most do—plan to exhaust heat from your cellar into your home's living space. The refrigeration unit should also either recover moisture from the cooled air with an internal condensation collector that allows condensation to evaporate again or use a split refrigeration system with an extra-large evaporator-to-condenser ratio to minimize the loss of humidity.

A split-refrigeration system has an evaporative coil mounted high on the cellar's wall and an outside condenser with a fan to dispel the heat. The two units are joined by a coolant line.

Refrigeration systems for wine cellars resemble whole-house air-conditioning systems, but they are specially designed and dedicated cooling systems able to ensure proper wine storage conditions. You'll likely need only a small-capacity, high-efficiency cooling unit to ensure an ideal environment in the heavily insulated, refrigerated wine room.

Select the system that best suits your cellar's location. There are three main types [see Specialized Cellar Equipment, page 126].

The first category includes self-contained, stand-alone, wall-mounted units that superficially resemble window-mounted air conditioners and vent through the wall into an adjacent space. While generally too noisy for use in areas where the cellar is adjacent to a bedroom, they are suitable for mounting next to a well-vented utility area, storage closet, laundry room, or unfinished spaces.

The second type of refrigeration systems is the split unit. A split-heat pump is ideal for a basement location. Its noisy condenser and fan are located outside the cellar, typically on the other side of a shared exterior wall.

The last category of cooler is an air-handling system. It is the best choice for a large cellar.

All cooling systems require you to run a new, dedicated circuit to the unit. Remember as you plan electrical circuits for your cellar that you will also need power for lighting and power outlets. For this, splice into existing wiring if a nearby circuit has sufficient capacity, or install new circuits specifically for the wine room.

Include a countertop, an island, or a table in your cellar to hold bottles, openers, decanters, and other service items. You'll find it useful as you select and open wines for your guests.

Though its primary purpose is wine storage, a well-built, functional wine room can also serve supplemental uses, including short-term storage of fine furs, bulk fruit and vegetables, cut flowers—or even cigars—all items that benefit from cool, humid climate conditions. Allow for these other uses in separate closets, cabinets, or side rooms within the wine room.

Finally, include a small island, table, or counter for opening or decanting wine or a quick sampling with a few guests—but plan adjacent space outside the cellar for extended dining and tasting parties.

Passive Cooling

For centuries, wine-makers have relied on caves and other below-grade or underground chambers to store and age wine. The 19th-century Far Niente winery in Oakville, California, for instance, features nearly 20,000 square feet of full-height caves and tunnels burrowed into the hill behind the facility, which provide naturally stable underground climate conditions to age wine. These caves were dug specifically with wine in mind.

Thermal mass and other passive cooling methods are far less reliable for an in-home cellar located in a basement or other below-grade space than are such deep, hillside caves. Seasonal climate changes cause temperature fluctuations in your home cellar and can harm your wine collection.

Use passive cooling as a supplement for active refrigeration [see Thermal Mass, page 112]. It also extends the life of refrigeration equipment by allowing it to run less frequently and for shorter periods of time than for rooms surrounded by higher temperature conditions, making your cellar cost less and saving energy.

EXTERIOR WALLS AND FOUNDATIONS

Your home's construction, along with the planned location of your wine cellar, are important factors in planning how your wine room will be built.

A brief overview of your home's main structural elements is essential before you begin constructing a home wine cellar.

- Does your home have a slab foundation, a raised perimeter foundation with a crawl space, or is it built on a basement foundation?
- Are the basement walls or foundation footings constructed of poured concrete, masonry blocks, bricks, or pressure-treated wood?
- Is the above-grade structure framed with wood or light-gauge steel?
- How are the existing exterior walls insulated and finished, and do they already have moisture barriers? How are the interior walls finished?
- What mechanical systems—electrical and plumbing—already exist, and can they accommodate expansion?

The answers to these questions set the stage for your building project, help decide your cellar's final location, determine the insulation and moisture barrier systems you'll need to add, and aid you as you upgrade the room's walls, floors, ceilings and electrical service, and add a refrigeration system.

Basement walls, for instance, often require you to add effective water and moisture vapor barriers. Understairs conversions might mean that the enamel paint and moisture-proof green-board finishing the walls of an adjacent bathroom can provide ample moisture barriers. Homes with slab or limited crawl-space foundations preclude below-grade wine cellars except as separate structures or additions—a new home or an addition, of course, allows you to build an ideal wine cellar.

With new construction, for instance, you could add a basement wine cellar, perhaps with its own staircase from the kitchen, butler's pantry, or family room above—even an adjacent entertainment area, secondary kitchen, or dining space.

While a slight premium may exist for upgraded insulation or other materials, equipment, or construction added to a new home, its cost can be amortized over the life of the structure's loan. Building a wine cellar as a retrofit to an existing home may actually entail higher, more immediate costs.

Remodeling an existing home to include a wine room may be challenging, but the actual skills needed are within most average homeowners' abilities to perform. Your home's structural components, mechanical services, and layout, specifically those that serve the wine cellar's chosen location, will likely require upgrading. Demolition may reveal hidden problems, such as dry rot, termites, or moisture damage; unexpected waste vents and drains; or the need for new structural bracing. You'll also remove wall finishes, open the walls to expose their framing, add insulation and moisture barriers if they are needed, install electricity, plumbing, and refrigeration systems, and finally restore the interior finish.

Outside, you may have to reroute gutters, provide new drains for rainwater, or excavate foundation walls to apply waterproofing and moisture membrane systems. You may also upgrade exterior insulation and vapor barrier membranes. In some cases you will have to route additional utility services from the existing main electrical panel, or even increase its capacity.

Prepare for such circumstances by learning about your home's construction, specifically its foundation and wall systems, as are discussed in the pages that follow.

Home exterior wall construction typically includes (A) outer siding, (B) waterproof flashing around all window and door openings, (C) water vapor and moisture barriers of building paper or other material, (D) plywood or oriented-strand-board sheathing, (E) fiberglass batt insulation, (F) structural framing, and (G) concrete foundation. The wall assembly is attached to the foundation with anchor bolts set in the concrete. Your home's construction may vary from the home shown in this illustration.

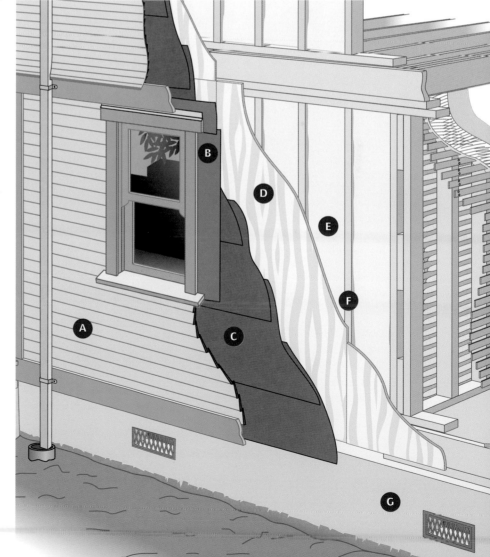

Slab Foundations

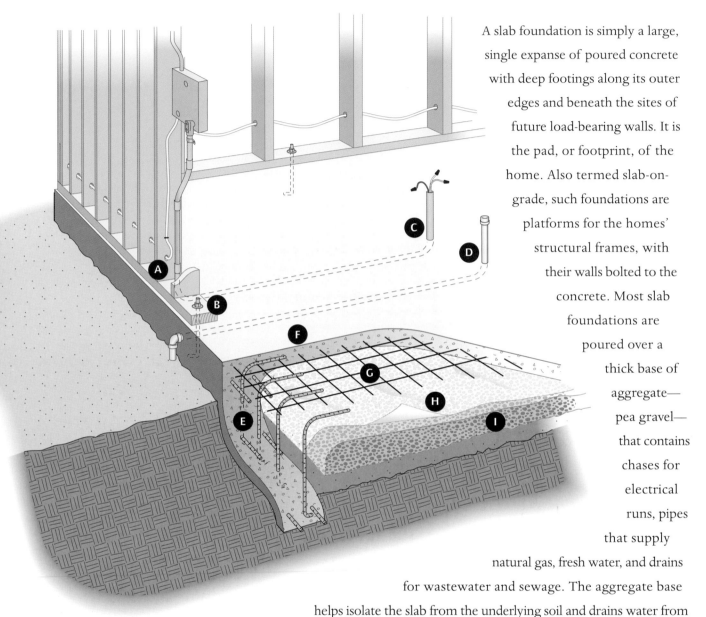

A slab foundation is simply a large, single expanse of poured concrete with deep footings along its outer edges and beneath the sites of future load-bearing walls. It is the pad, or footprint, of the home. Also termed slab-on-grade, such foundations are platforms for the homes' structural frames, with their walls bolted to the concrete. Most slab foundations are poured over a thick base of aggregate—pea gravel—that contains chases for electrical runs, pipes that supply natural gas, fresh water, and drains for wastewater and sewage. The aggregate base helps isolate the slab from the underlying soil and drains water from its underside. It also mitigates hydrostatic pressure that can cause cracks and leaks in the slab. Slab foundations are ideal for areas with expansive soils that hinder effective below-grade drainage and will damage full-basement foundations.

Slab foundations are easier, faster, and more economical to build than either perimeter raised-floor foundations or full-basement foundations. While they rule out the possibility of building or adding a wine cellar below grade, their massive concrete pads add significant amounts of thermal mass to the floor of above-ground wine rooms.

Components of slab foundations include (A) wall baseplate or sill and studs, (B) anchor bolts, (C) wiring chase and stub-out, (D) plumbing stub-out, (E) reinforced perimeter concrete footing poured contiguous with (F) a monolithic slab, (G) wire mesh or steel reinforcement bars, (H) moisture barrier, and (I) compacted aggregate base.

Raised-Floor Perimeter Foundations

Also referred to as crawl space foundations, raised-floor perimeter foundations feature short concrete or masonry block walls that define the home's perimeter footprint, with mud sills and rim joists that support a wood-framed floor set two to four feet (60 to 120 cm) above the earth (or grade). The space between the floor joists and the ground is called the crawl space. It often includes short concrete piers and wooden posts that support the floor joists under bearing walls at strategic midspan locations. Inside the perimeter may be other poured concrete footings that support heavy bearing loads from the structure above.

A crawl space provides a convenient and out-of-sight location with easy access for heating and cooling ducts, plumbing pipes, and electrical wire conduits. The soil beneath the house may be covered with plastic sheeting or waterproofing membrane to block moisture vapor that condenses on the floor joists and causes decay or the growth of mold. In cold-winter climates, the space between the floor joists is often insulated with rigid foam, sprayed-on cellulose, or fiberglass batt blankets, but in other climate conditions, you may have to add insulation between the floor joists under your wine room.

Like slabs, raised-floor foundations generally preclude below-grade wine rooms. You may have to add bracing to support the floor joists in the wine room to carry the added static weight of its many bottles. Sheltered crawl spaces can also be used for short-term, ambient-temperature wine storage of full cases. The major drawbacks are limited capacity and difficult access to the wine.

Components of a raised-floor perimeter foundation include (A) undisturbed or compacted soil, (B) steel-reinforced concrete footings, (C) perimeter foundation walls, (D) air vents, (E) anchor bolts, (F) sill plate, (G) rim joist for attaching the floor joists, and (H) wall studs. Some raised-floor perimeter foundations have foundation walls made of concrete blocks and concrete piers to support bearing walls and furnaces located inside the structure.

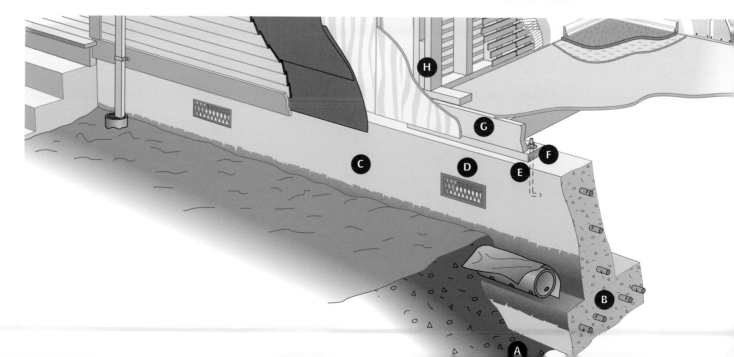

Basements and Subterranean Construction

A full basement is the only foundation type that allows a walk-in, below-grade wine cellar, unless you excavate and convert an existing raised-floor perimeter foundation [see Converting a Crawl Space, below]. About half of all homes have full-height basements with an approximately 80-inch (203-cm) clearance between a typical concrete slab floor and the structure's first-floor joists.

Basement walls are either poured concrete or stacked masonry blocks—also called CMUs—filled with concrete and strengthened with steel reinforcement bars. Poured concrete fills temporary wood-panel forms that shape the footings and walls of the concrete until it cures. The forms are removed once the concrete hardens, leaving only the monolithic concrete walls of the basement.

Converting a Crawl Space

It's possible, though laborious, to excavate and build a full-height basement within a crawl space foundation; for a wine cellar, it might be prohibitively expensive. The project could be more easily justified and would add more value to your home if your excavated basement project includes other amenities or allows for uses beyond the wine cellar, such as for a laundry, a guest or family room, or a home theater.

In block walls, workers stack and mortar CMU blocks prior to the concrete grout, fit reinforcing bars inside their open cells, and fill their voids with concrete. Jointed-masonry walls are more susceptible to ground-water intrusion than is poured concrete; both types of wall should have an exterior moisture barrier membrane and a subsurface drain system to keep the cellar truly dry.

Another modern concrete foundation wall system—insulated concrete forms, or ICFs—acts as a poured wall's formwork. It avoids building and removing temporary forms. It also provides built-in, permanent, rigid-foam insulation on both sides of a steel-reinforced, poured concrete wall, and it delivers superior insulation compared to concrete alone.

All these masonry systems provide high levels of thermal mass—the ability to retard the transfer of heat and cold through the wall.

Occasionally, builders use pressure-treated, rot-resistant wood framing and sheathing for basement walls. These are called permanent wood foundations, or PWFs, and are thought to be faster to build and less expensive than concrete or masonry foundation systems. Like above-grade wood-framed walls, PWF construction makes for easy wall cavity insulation installation and finishing.

Regardless of construction type, basement walls are either partially or completely below grade. Their exterior surfaces should be sheathed to protect them from water infiltration and, if groundwater is present, drains should be installed above and around the perimeter footing [see Correcting Poor Drainage, page 102, and Installing French Drains, page 104].

Stairs inside the home from the floor above typically provide access to a basement, though they frequently also have cellar doors for fire exits, as required by many building codes. Most basements also have hopper or casement windows set in protected wells; they provide significant natural light and fresh air from the outside as well as another escape route. If you are designing a new home with a full basement, consider installing a secondary, dedicated staircase within your home to the basement. It will give you convenient access to your collection.

It's also best to locate the wine room in a corner of the basement to take advantage of the thermal mass qualities of the soil-sheltered perimeter walls. They moderate temperature swings, will help create and maintain ideal cellar conditions, and also reduce your budget for building the cellar.

Components of a subterranean basement foundation can include (A) site of future wine room adjacent to two exterior walls, (B) provision for diverting runoff water from the foundation, (C) waterproof basement window dam, (D) moisture barrier membrane to block infiltrating water, (E) plastic water barrier preventing water from entering basement wall, (F) pea gravel to collect groundwater, (G) perforated drainpipe to collect and channel water, (H) sump pump to remove water, (I) reinforced concrete footing, (J) poured concrete wall, (K) reinforced concrete block wall, and (L) poured concrete basement floor.

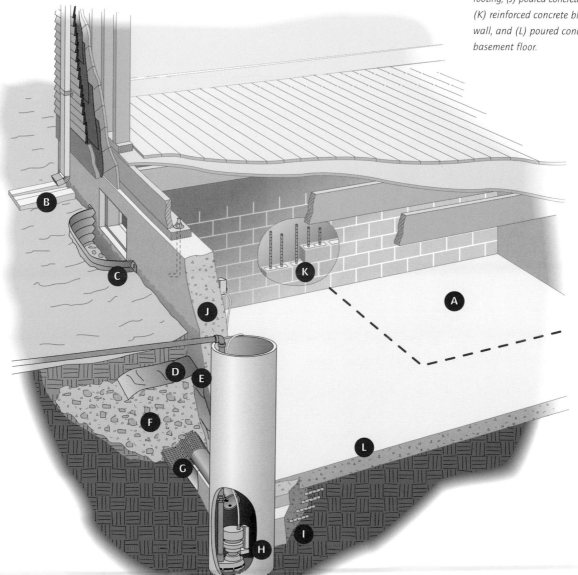

Above-Grade Masonry Walls

Occasionally, builders use CMU blocks for part or all of a home's above-grade exterior walls. Though the masonry blocks lack the earth-sheltering protection of a subterranean wall, above-grade masonry walls offer greater thermal mass than wood-framed walls. This thermal mass effect can be further increased if you insulate the walls on one or both sides and clad them with exterior stucco or masonry veneer.

Special construction techniques are necessary to attach conventional gypsum wallboard or paneling to masonry, compared to a wood-framed wall. To create an insulation cavity and a nailing surface for the wall finish, attach wood slats or studs—called furring strips—to the masonry or build a standard frame wall and tilt it up against the masonry wall, fastening it in place with concrete anchors. Place high-density, rigid insulation in bays between the furring strips or fill the cavities of the stud wall with fiberglass batts. A moisture barrier should be applied to the exterior of the wall.

Components of an above-grade masonry wall constructed of CMU blocks include (A) reinforced, poured concrete footing, (B) steel reinforcement bars in each concrete-filled void of the CMU blocks, (C) mortared joints, (D) mud sill with anchor bolts set into concrete in the CMU block voids, (E) cripple stud wall to span between the masonry wall to the second-floor joists, and (F) a concrete slab floor. Your home may have masonry walls from the footings to the floor joists instead of the partial wooden stud wall shown here.

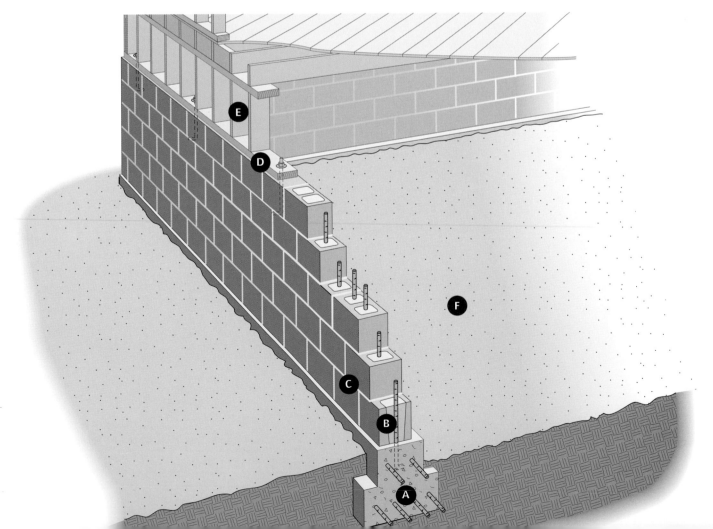

Wood-Framed Interior Walls

Most new and existing homes feature wood wall and roof framing systems. With timber resources in abundant supply, builders use lumber for every above-grade framing component, including sill and top plates, wall studs, headers, beams, posts, floor and roof joists, and roof rafters and trusses. Wood remains the most efficient material for construction in terms of time, cost, and resources.

Like masonry construction, wood-framed walls in a wine cellar need additional insulation to provide thermal mass. Fill each stud cavity with insulation or apply it to the wall surface, fill every opening, and install water and vapor barriers to keep it dry [see Interior Wall Vapor Barriers, page 114].

Building thermally efficient walls helps control your wine cellar's climate. It's easy to upgrade to the highest level—or R-value—of insulation, seal each penetration, and attach a continuous vapor barrier to effectively block moisture infiltration. It's also simple and quick to attach wallboard and finishes such as paneling or racking systems to wood-framed walls, compared to masonry walls.

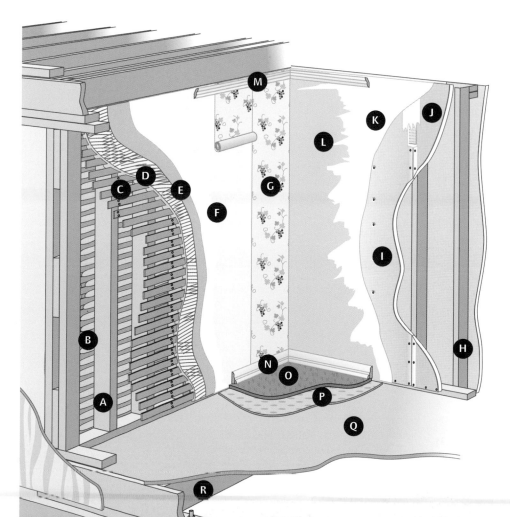

Different types of finishes used for common types of wood-framed walls are shown in this illustration.

The components of a plaster wall are (A) wooden frame studs, (B) lath with plaster "keys" protruding through it, (C) lath to support plaster, (D) plaster brown coat, (E) plaster top coat, (F) wallpaper sizing, and (G) wallpaper.

The components of a wallboard wall are (H) wooden frame studs, (I) gypsum wallboard, (J) wallboard joint compound and tape, (K) spackle, (L) primer and paint, and (M) crown molding.

The components of a floor system include (N) baseboard molding, (O) carpet, (P) pad, (Q) subfloor, and (R) floor joists.

CORRECTING POOR DRAINAGE

For both new and existing homes, drain rainwater runoff away from the foundation to the property's lowest point or to the street. This eliminates groundwater collecting to produce hydrostatic pressure against the basement walls that causes cracks and forces water into your crawl space or basement.

Proper drainage away from your structure begins with sloping the soil around it to carry rain and runoff away from the foundation. Divert water by grading slopes in the soil leading away from all sides of the house; add fill and regrade the site, as necessary.

Determine the lowest points of grade on your property or find the direction in which water naturally flows from it. Direct water to these points with surface channels or by installing subterranean drains. The drainpipes can emerge from the soil at the low point or be attached to outlets at the street that permit the water to enter a storm sewer.

Install, replace, and adjust gutters with a slope of two inches (50 mm) in ten feet (3 m) to carry water to downspouts. It's ideal if downspouts terminate near the lowest point of grade on the lot.

Downspouts located at higher points may require you to install below-grade drain lines of four-inch (10-cm) ABS flexible pipe leading to rigid underground runs of PVC pipe. Extend the pipe from the end of the downspout to a drain system leading to the lowest point of grade. With the connections in place, water runoff will flow away from the house and your foundation will remain dry.

If you use surface channels to carry away downspout water, extend the downspouts at least two feet (60 cm) away from the house, install splash blocks to prevent erosion and water absorption into the soil, and direct the water away from the house toward the low point or to the runoff channel.

Follow these steps to achieve proper gutter, downspout, and drainage systems.

STEP 1

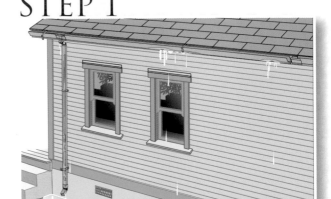

Examine the perimeter of your home. Water beneath structures or in basements is caused by leaking, deteriorating, or broken gutters and downspouts. Standing water near the foundation's edge results from improper grading. Either condition can damage siding or sheathing and cause the foundation to settle, crack, or leak.

STEP 4

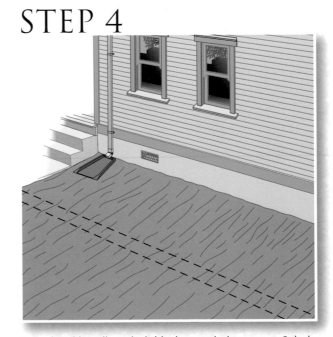

Extend and install a splash block at each downspout. Splash blocks made of cast concrete should extend at least 18" (45 cm) from the foundation. Clear a channel from the splash block to the location where you will install subsurface drains.

STEP 2

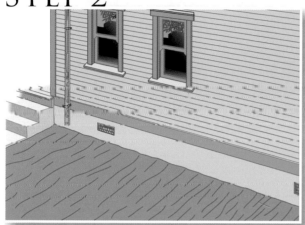

Begin the correction process by regrading the soil surface surrounding your structure. When you finish, it should start well below the foundation vents or basement windows and slope away from the structure. Allow at least 4″ (10 cm) of fall for each 24″ (60 cm) of distance.

STEP 3

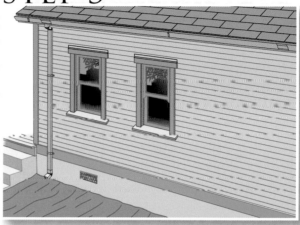

Repair or replace leaky gutters, sealing joints between the gutter sections. Install new downspout diverters, and patch or replace any rusty sections. Use a hose to check the proper operation of all gutters and downspouts when you finish.

STEP 5

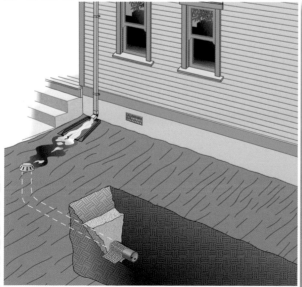

Dig a trench and install 4″ (10-cm) perforated PVC pipe wrapped in porous landscape fabric at its base. Backfill the trench with gravel to 12″ (30 cm) below its top surface. Complete the backfill with loose, humus-rich soil.

STEP 6

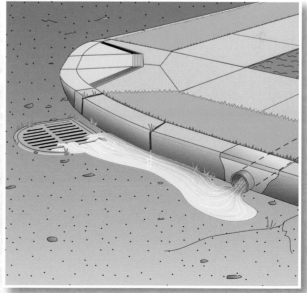

Connect the drainpipe to a curb outlet or run it to daylight, allowing it to carry the runoff water to a municipal storm sewer or a natural watercourse.

INSTALLING FRENCH DRAINS

Because groundwater in the soil around a basement or foundation gains pressure with soil depth unless you already have an effective drain system, remedying leaks from inside of the structure seldom is successful. The water pressure forces caulk out of cracks and liquid through porous concrete. Rather, install a so-called French drain around the perimeter of the foundation or basement wall to collect runoff and groundwater, directing it away from the structure. The combination of a French drain and an external water barrier membrane will solve leaking basement problems in most situations.

The installation process requires considerable effort and is best performed with heavy earth-moving equipment. You will excavate a wide trench in the soil around your home to the top of its foundation's footings. In a full basement, this can mean removing soil up to ten feet (3 m) deep in a trench as wide as 6 feet (1.8 m). Always obtain all the necessary approvals and permits required in your jurisdiction, and consult with a licensed professional engineer for advice and plans before installing a foundation French drain.

Exercise caution when working in an excavated trench, especially if the surrounding soil is saturated. Slumping and sudden collapse is a personal hazard.

Despite the scale of the project, French drains are simple in concept and operation. Water collects in the pipe after filtering down through a layer of surrounding pea gravel. It then drains away to a sump pump, a surface outlet, a storm drain, or another release point.

The project will require several weekends to excavate the trench, apply waterproofing membrane, lay the pipe, install a pump, and backfill the excavation with aggregate and soil. You'll need average skills and tools, and you may want to rent a miniature backhoe or other equipment to speed your task.

The steps shown here depict a general situation in which most of the water is caused by runoff; the conditions found on your site may vary. If your home is built on a site with a high groundwater table, additional waterproofing measures and pump systems may be required to eliminate leaks in your basement.

STEP 1

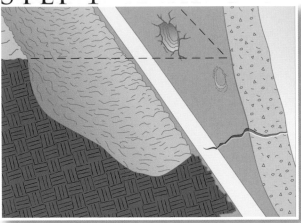

Excavate to the top of the basement's foundation footings. Avoid disturbing soil beneath the foundation; footings should always remain on undisturbed soil. Slope the trench's open side, preventing slumping and giving yourself ample space to work.

STEP 4

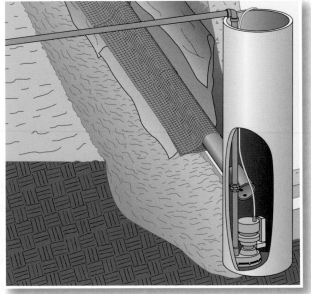

Install perforated PVC drain pipe wrapped in porous landscape fabric along the top of the foundation footing. Slope the pipe 4" (10 cm) every 10' (3 m), with its perforations positioned at the pipe's bottom. Run the pipe to daylight, or install a submersible sump pump to extract drain water.

STEP 2

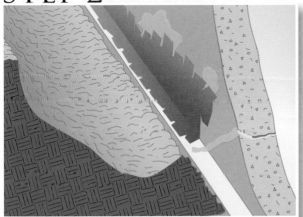

Clean the foundation wall, removing clinging soil and roots. Use patching concrete to fill any voids, cracks, or spalls in the foundation, and allow it to dry. Apply plastic water-proofing compound to the entire surface of the wall from its base to at least 6" (15 cm) above the planned level of the soil surface.

STEP 3

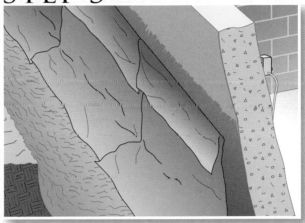

While the mastic is still moist, apply 6 mil (0.15 mm) plastic sheeting to the wall. Attach the plastic to the wall from its footing to 6" (15 cm) below the planned soil surface, with a loose flap extending at least 2' (60 cm) beyond. Overlap plastic panels at least 16" (41 cm), sealing joints with mastic.

STEP 5

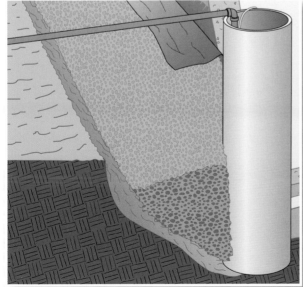

Backfill the trench with pea gravel, with the aggregate just to the top attachment of the moisture barrier. Grade the aggregate to slope away from the foundation, then fold the flap of plastic sheeting over it to drain water away from the foundation wall.

STEP 6

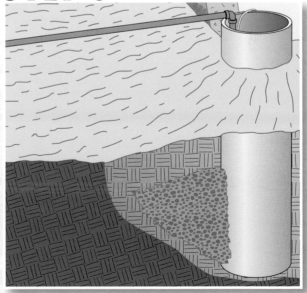

Backfill the remainder of the trench with topsoil, covering the surface in a layer 6"–8" (15–20 cm) deep. At the foundation, it should be 2"–4" (50–100 mm) below the mastic. Grade the soil in a slope that will carry surface runoff water away from the foundation.

Exterior-Wall Vapor Barriers

Moisture vapor barriers and waterproof membranes stop wind-driven rain and other sources of water and moisture from infiltrating exterior walls, soaking their insulation, reducing their thermal values, even leading to mold, rot, and structural collapse. Both types of barriers have value in exterior wall construction. A moisture vapor barrier stops water from passing through, both in its liquid and its gaseous form. A waterproof membrane, by contrast, stops the flow of water into your walls even if it is under pressure.

Most above-grade exterior walls are protected by moisture vapor barriers, while those partially or totally underground require both a vapor and a water barrier. Some barrier membranes allow water in gaseous form to pass through them; they are intended for use where moisture must escape through the walls of the house. In a wine cellar, an impermeable barrier should be applied to the warm side of the exterior wall or, if the wall experiences varied climate conditions, barrier protection on both its inner and outer surfaces. This requirement varies from standard building practices that leave the inside wall free to breathe.

Two types of moisture can affect your home's and cellar's walls. The first of these is water from rain or runoff. You should weatherproof all of your exterior walls to stop water from entering them. Enamel paint is one primary defense; the other is an unbroken moisture barrier mounted between the siding, facing, or stucco and the subsurface sheathing.

The second type of moisture is generated by condensation of water vapor. Water condenses from warm, moist air when it encounters a cool surface—the same effect you see on the sides of a glass filled with a cold beverage. Because water vapor travels through porous materials with the same ease as air, including wallboard and paneling, condensation can occur inside your walls as easily as on their surfaces. It is also hard to detect condensation within walls.

The goal when you build your wine cellar is to block all water vapor from entering the wall cavities that contain the cellar's insulation. When moisture barriers fail and condensation forms inside a wall, it is absorbed by the insulation. This reduces its insulating properties, and the amount of condensation increases. Over time, the insulation becomes saturated and mold and mildew set in. Over even longer periods, the wall's studs will begin to decay and the structure will fail. It's very important to stop these things from happening before they start.

A breathable vapor barrier behind your home's siding combined with a waterproof membrane will stop both liquid and gaseous water from penetrating the exterior walls of your wine cellar. In climates where outside temperatures are consistently warmer than the living space, most home's walls will have a water barrier on their exterior side. If you live in a so-called heating climate where the exterior of your house is nearly always cooler than its interior, your home will likely have a water barrier under the exterior wall's interior side rather than behind its siding. Mixed climates may have either protection, or neither.

Plan to examine your walls during construction of your wine cellar to confirm the presence of a moisture barrier on any adjacent exterior walls. If you find that the barrier is missing, plan to install one before you insulate and refinish the walls of your cellar. Follow the guidelines given above depending on the climate in which you live, or obtain professional advice from a knowledgeable expert familiar with moisture barriers for your area.

Components of an exterior wall of a wine cellar include (A) exterior siding protected by enamel paint, (B) foil-clad rigid-foam insulation and vapor barrier, (C) foil-taped joints, (D) oriented-strand board or plywood sheathing, (E) wall studs, (F) fiberglass-batt insulation with its kraft face to exterior of wall, and (G) wallboard.

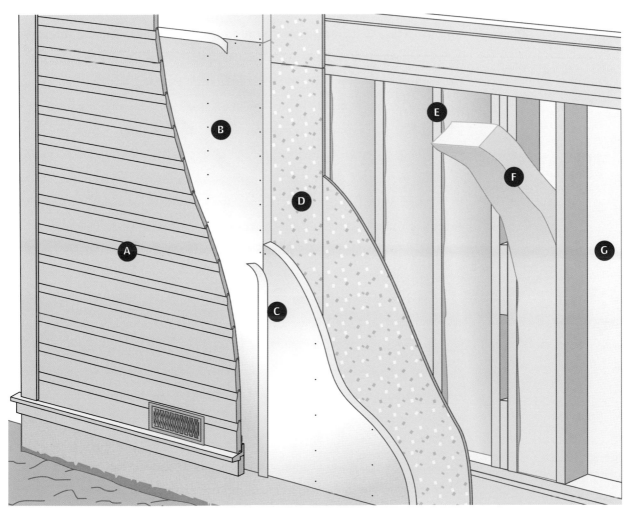

WINE CELLAR UTILITIES

Plan to provide the equipment and fixtures of your wine cellar and its adjacent areas with power and other utilities before construction begins.

Electrical Systems

Home wine cellars require various utilities or mechanical connections depending on the scope or features of the project. Every cellar, however, needs a dedicated and adequate source of electricity, primarily to power the refrigeration system and the lighting fixtures.

Electrical requirements for refrigeration systems vary by the model and the capacity rating of the stand-alone, split refrigeration, or air-handling system you select for your wine room. Plan at least for a 115-volt, 20-amp dedicated circuit run with 12-gauge, three-wire cable from the main electrical service panel, though some large cellars may need more than one 115-volt or a 220-volt circuits. Provide additional outlets, junction boxes, switches, and wiring, either from the same circuit or another dedicated line, for lighting fixtures, wall outlets, and other electrical needs. Plan also to run wire from the refrigeration system to the location of the thermostat that controls it if it is not hard-wired to the unit. Always read completely and comply with all electrical code and permit requirements when planning and installing electrical service components, or rely on the services of a licensed profession electrician.

A dedicated circuit serving the wine cellar ensures that only the refrigeration system will draw power from the circuit, providing a reliable source, free of interruptions. Troubleshooting is similarly easy to diagnose on an isolated circuit.

Most wine refrigeration systems designed for large-capacity (600-plus-bottle) cellars are hard-wired to an electrical circuit, while smaller units are usually plugged into outlets. Once you determine the right cooling system and its size and location in the wine cellar, run wiring to that location through the home's structural frame, or use flexible or rigid electrical conduit with enough slack (and extra wire) to connect it to the cooling equipment inside a surface-mounted electrical junction box. Remember that part of the equipment for an air-handling or split system is located at a remote—usually exterior—location away from the cellar room.

An air-handling system also requires vents and ducting at recommended locations high on the walls of the cellar to extract air, cool it by circulating it through the heat exchanger, and exhaust it into the room to maintain the wine room's desired temperature and climate. Such systems are complex, and you should consult a heating, ventilation, and air-conditioning specialist for assistance in planning and routing ductwork for an air-handling system in a wine cellar.

Components of a wine cellar's electrical system are (A) main electrical service panel, (B) refrigeration system and dedicated circuit outlet, (C) junction box with track lighting, (D) junction box with overhead lighting fixture, (E) lighting timer and dimmer switches for the wine room and butler's pantry room, (F) outlets, and (G) junction box.

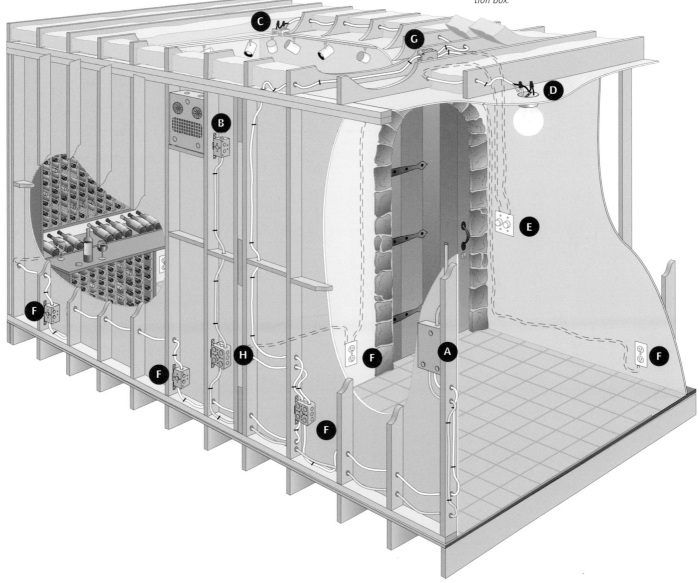

Water and Plumbing Systems

In addition to their electrical connections, both split refrigeration and air-handling systems also require drain lines that collect condensation generated by the cooling system. The condensation gathers in an open reservoir within the cellar, where it can evaporate to replenish the room's humidity, is discharged out-of-doors, or routed to flow into a wastewater drain. Running drain lines is a small plumbing job that may also include installing separate humidity equipment to maintain adequate levels of moisture for storing wine.

Grand wine cellars with built-in bar sinks and faucets require even more extensive levels of plumbing systems. It's best to provide a sink in an adjacent butler's pantry or other nearby service room equipped with running water to keep from introducing excess moisture into the cellar. Always avoid installing appliances such as dishwashers in the cellar; they can generate heat and vibration as they operate, both detrimental to proper wine storage and aging. For these plumbing attachments, you must typically extend your home's existing hot and cold supply water and wastewater lines to the sink or appliance location.

The supply-water system consists of a cold-water supply pipe and one for hot water. Locate the existing "water walls" of your home; most houses are built with plumbing clustered into a few locations. You can recognize a water wall by its adjacent location to existing sinks or the presence of vent stacks on the roof. They are generally found in one wall of a kitchen, bathroom, or laundry room, and you'll tap into the lines in one of these locations to provide water to your wine storage area.

Pipes can run through stud walls, beneath or over floor and ceiling joists, and through soffits and chases that contain HVAC ducts. Surface mounts are necessary for most masonry walls.

Installing wastewater pipes means making a connection to an existing sewer drain line and providing a vent stack to relieve pressure and dispel sewer gases, either as new construction or by tapping into an existing vent.

Consider installing personalized and unique plumbing fixtures that extend the decorating theme of your wine cellar, such as this wine-barrel faucet and sink.

Components of a plumbing system in a butler's pantry include (A) hot-water supply line from the home's water heater, (B) cold-water supply line, (C) shutoff valves, (D) temperature-mixing faucet, (E) sink, (F) sink drain with P-trap, (G) spur wastewater line, (H) main sewer line and vent stack leading to municipal sewer or septic tank, and (I) sink auxiliary vent stack.

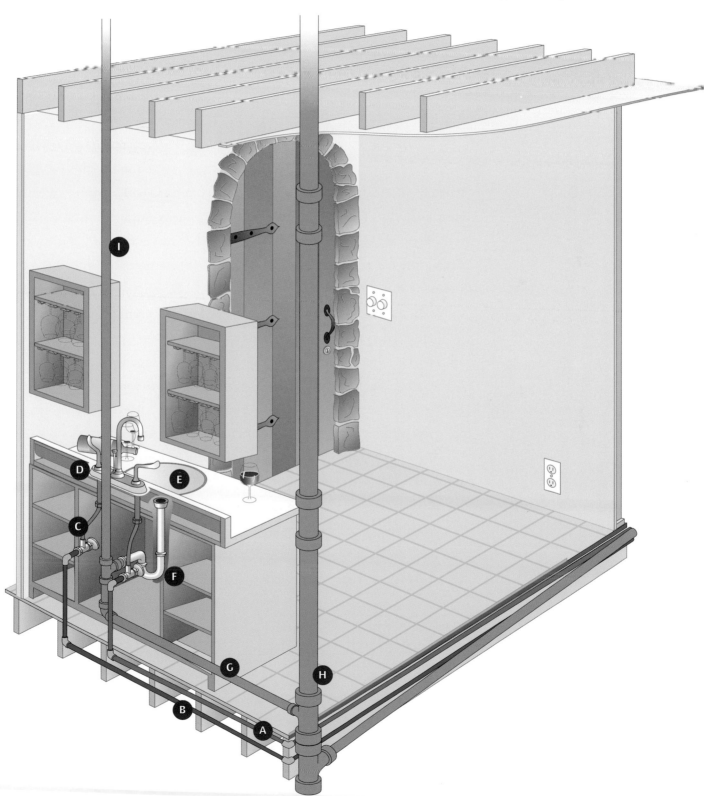

THERMAL MASS

The dense ceramic tile, brick, concrete, and stone components of your cellar's wall and floor finishes are more than for window dressing. They help keep its temperature even.

Opposite page: More than simple decorative elements treasured for their beauty alone, the stones in this arch and the natural flagstone floor underfoot help keep the air temperature of this cellar constant. The dense stones absorb heat and release it slowly, keeping the temperature steady.

Retarding the transfer of heat and cold through the wine cellar walls is essential to maintaining a desired and ideal climate inside the room. While insulating the walls, floor, and ceiling slows the transfer of energy into and out of the cellar, you should also include masonry finishes to provide thermal mass to absorb and release heat, moderating changes in temperature. Building or remodeling walls with a combination of materials supplements your insulation and provides a store for thermal energy.

Masonry foundation walls in a basement provide excellent thermal mass qualities [see Basements and Subterranean Construction, page 98]. The masonry in these walls slowly absorbs heat as they warm and releases it as they cool, moderating temperature changes in the surrounding air. Above-grade masonry walls have the same thermal mass benefits, though they lack the cooling effects of soil surrounding them [see Above-grade Masonry Walls, page 100]. Thermal mass can also work against you, adding heat from walls or floors exposed to sunlight.

Wood-framed walls, by contrast to masonry walls, rely mainly on their stud cavity and surface foam insulation to limit temperature change. These materials effectively retard thermal transfer through the structure, but you can enhance their benefit by adding dense finishes. Gypsum wallboard, or drywall, on the inside faced in stone and a masonry exterior finish, such as brick, fiber cement siding, stucco, or stone, enhance the wall's thermal mass capabilities.

Add ceramic, marble, or slate tiles, or other natural stone finishes to the cellar's floor to further increase your cellar's thermal mass. Masonry floors are helpful for adding thermal mass in cellars installed on the second floor or those built on the raised floors of a perimeter foundation.

INTERIOR-WALL VAPOR BARRIERS

OPTION A

Block water and moisture vapor from entering the insulation surrounding your wine cellar through shared exterior and interior walls, and keep the relative humidity constant within your wine storage area. Our breath and perspiration, plus the acts of cooking, bathing, washing clothes, and many other daily activities, all release water. In your walls, liquid water condenses from water vapor at the point where it encounters the cool conditions of your cellar.

The general rule followed by most building experts is to place moisture barriers as close as possible to the surface of the warm side of a wall. They apply tarlike barrier coatings, flashings, impermeable building paper, and high-tech vapor barriers such as Tyvek® under the siding or stucco on a home's exterior walls. Interior walls, by contrast, seldom have a moisture barrier unless they enclose a bathroom, laundry area, or kitchen.

Your wine cellar will be kept cool compared to the living area of your home. Because of this, it should have an unbroken moisture barrier surrounding all of its walls, ceiling, and floor. On exterior walls that already have a moisture barrier over their sheathing or under their siding, it's a good idea to add an interior moisture barrier as well. Since your cellar will have a relatively high humidity level and the exterior walls may be even cooler than the cellar for months or years at a time, this second moisture barrier will keep the insulation that they contain dry and efficient. It will also prevent fungal spores from sprouting inside the walls and causing mildew and rot.

There are several different approaches to creating a moisture barrier around your wine cellar. Select the most appropriate and effective method for your site, the construction of your cellar, its location in your home, and the presence of any shared walls.

Applying a moisture barrier as you build your cellar takes a few hours at most. Retrofitting a moisture barrier is a major task that can require removing all of your racks and furnishings as well as your cellar's wallboard before you begin the actual application.

Weave 6 mil (0.15 mm) plastic sheeting in and out of the stud cavities prior to installing fiberglass batt insulation. Fasten the plastic sheet to the back of the wall cavity with spray adhesive and hold it in place at the back of the studs with staples. It's easiest to cut a large roll of plastic film into lengths and apply it progressively, starting at a top corner, working down each cavity, then proceeding to the next cavity. Work carefully, avoiding punctures, tears, or rips; overlap all joints at least 2″ (50 mm), and seal any holes, including those made by staples. Where fire-blocking creates an obstacle, cut the main plastic sheet to fit it around the blocking, then overlay it with a patch set in adhesive.

OPTION B

Install kraft-faced fiberglass-batt insulation with its kraft face and moisture barrier facing toward the outside of the structure. Make cuts in the batt and fill any voids behind pipes, blocking, or electrical wires. If there are penetrations from recessed light fixtures, outlet boxes, switches, plumbing vent stacks or other in-wall fixtures, use expanding foam to seal every hole. Remember to fill the spaces between studs at corners, in knotholes, or where wood splits leave gaps. Your goal is to fill every cavity with insulation, whether it is fiberglass batt, rigid foam, or expandable foam. Use water-proof construction tape to join runs of batt insulation, over-lapping the kraft paper before you apply the tape.

OPTION C

For wine cellars that share adjacent walls with another interior space, paint the walls in those rooms with several coats of a waterproof enamel paint to create a moisture barrier on the extreme outside of the shared wall, away from the cellar.

OPTION D

If the exposed wall cavity has too many pipes, wires, or ducts running through it, or if it is too narrow to properly install plastic sheeting or kraft-faced insulation, paint the back-side of the drywall or sheathing and studs with waterproof enamel paint, using a sprayer or aerosol can.

Insulation

Applying insulation to the surface or the cavities of a wall slows the transfer of heat through that wall. The thermal ability of any insulation material is measured by its R-value (or resistance to thermal transfer); the higher the R-value, the better its performance. Take care as you install any insulation material, but especially fiberglass batts, to ensure it retains its full R-value in the structure; stuffing, folding, compacting, or otherwise compressing batts in a wall cavity as you wrap them around pipes and wiring, for instance, significantly reduces its insulating potential [see Fiberglass Batt Insulation, page 119].

In a wine cellar, plan to apply higher insulation values in the walls, floor, and ceiling—combined with air-tightness to reduce leakage that further transfers heat through the structure—to keep the room at a steady temperature. Typical batt insulation for 2×4 wall construction is rated at R-13, though denser material achieves a slightly higher value, about R-15, for common wall cavities. Thicker walls, built of 2×6 and 2×8 frame components, allow even higher R-values, up to R-19 and R-22. You can increase these R-values still further by adding surface insulation in the form of rigid foam [see Rigid-Foam Insulation, page 118].

Below: Where your wine cellar's walls contain access holes for wiring runs, plumbing pipes, ducts, or other equipment, seal them with penetrating, expanding foam.

Bottom: Both fiberglass batt and high-density rigid foam insulation are available with or without a moisture barrier. Only a single moisture barrier should be applied in interior walls; exterior walls should have a moisture barrier beneath both their interior and exterior surfaces.

Several materials are appropriate for effective structural insulation of a wine cellar, though the most common is fiberglass batts—rolls of spun fiberglass, either with or without a kraft-paper vapor-barrier face on one side. Fiberglass batts are appropriate for wall, ceiling, and floor insulation. Install them between the studs in a wall cavity, between the joists in the floor, and between the rafters in the roof.

Fiberglass and cellulose fiber, a mixture of recycled paper and pulp, also can be "blown in" loose, most commonly in attic spaces, to achieve even greater coverage—especially around heating ducts, water pipes, and wiring—and often higher R-values. On a horizontal surface, such as between the joists of a ceiling, either loose-fill material can be blown in a layer higher than the top of the joists to achieve R-values well above R-20.

Fired though a pneumatic gun from a hopper, cellulose fiber is either mixed with adhesive and applied wet, or it is shot dry and contained in the wall and joist cavities by plastic sheeting or simple gravity. Like loose-fill fiberglass, cellulose insulation offers more complete coverage in the cavity, helping the insulation system to retain its designed R-value. Wet cellulose dries quickly; it is then held in place by wallboard or paneling. Both wet and dry cellulose contain recycled content—typically cardboard boxes or newspapers—making them an environmentally sound choice, as well.

Rigid, high-density foam insulation, in the form of panels fastened to the walls or ceiling in the same manner as plywood sheathing, offer a dense insulation product with somewhat lower R-values than batts or other cavity insulation options. Rigid-foam insulation panels may supplement fiberglass batt cavity insulation, and when it is finished with a foil face, can also serve as a vapor barrier. For wine cellars in climates subject to significant temperature swings, consider installing supplemental rigid-foam insulation on the inside faces of the rooms' interior walls and ceilings [see Rigid-Foam Insulation, page 118]. Rigid-foam insulation also can be installed between the exterior wall studs and its sheathing.

When insulating a wine cellar, always opt for the most insulation possible in any situation. Higher R-values in your walls, ceilings, and floors means lower refrigeration cost, less wear and tear on equipment, and fewer maintenance calls or system failures requiring replacement.

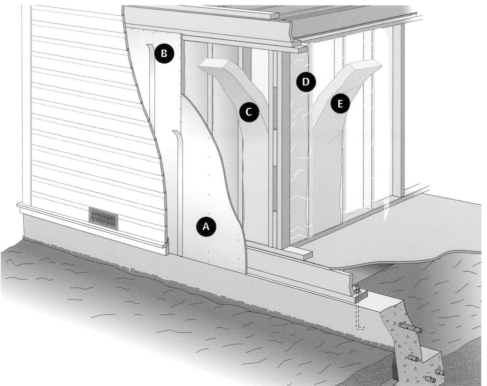

Components of a wine cellar's insulation systems in an exterior wall are (A) foil-faced rigid-foam surface insulation beneath the siding, (B) sealed joints that prevent moisture penetration from the outside through the wall, (C) fiberglass-batt insulation in the exterior wall cavity with its kraft face facing the outside.

Components of the insulation systems for an interior wall of a wine cellar are (D) plastic moisture barrier woven around the studs, and (E) fiberglass-batt insulation without a kraft face in the interior wall cavity. (In this illustration, the wine cellar is on the opposite side of the interior wall.)

RIGID-FOAM INSULATION

High-density, rigid-foam insulation provides an easy-to-install insulation material for ceilings and walls. When its joints are sealed with tape, it also helps block the travel of air and moisture vapor through the structure, supplementing the walls' moisture barriers.

Rigid foam is the best choice for ceilings because it is lightweight and easy to handle and attach. It also can be mounted over existing surfaces, attached to studs outside the wall cavities, or installed under wooden paneling.

Follow these steps and options to properly install high-density rigid-foam-insulation panels.

PREPARATION

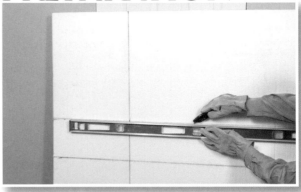

Mark and cut the foam to fit the cavities or spans required.

CEILINGS

For ceilings, fasten panels to joists using deck screws and plastic retaining washers. Note the plastic vapor barrier.

WALLS: STEP 1

In wall cavities, generously apply panel adhesive to the foam boards with a caulking gun.

WALLS: STEP 2

Position the panels in the cavity, square them, and press them into the adhesive.

WALLS: STEP 3

Tape all joints following the manufacturer's directions. Tape the spaces between the panels and the wall studs.

FIBERGLASS-BATT INSULATION

Fiberglass-batt insulation is the most common material used to insulate walls, ceilings, and floors. Install the material properly, to avoid creating voids or compressing the batts in the wall or joist cavities.

Batt insulation is the best choice for deep-cavity walls constructed with 2 × 6 and 2 × 8 members. If an effective moisture barrier is already in place, or if you are installing batts in multiple layers, choose a batt without a kraft-paper face. Only one kraft face should exist within a wall cavity.

Follow these steps to install fiberglass-batt insulation in walls and under stairways.

PREPARATION

Choose batts to fit your wall cavity. Cut them to length.

WALLS: STEP 1

Make cuts in the batt and fit it loosely around wires, pipes, ducts, and other obstacles. Avoid compacting the batt.

WALLS: STEP 2

If the batts slump in the wall cavity, staple a tautly stretched string across the stud faces to hold it in place.

STAIRS: STEP 1

In understairs cellars, install a first layer of kraft-free batt in each riser-and-tread cavity over the moisture barrier.

STAIRS: STEP 2

With the first layer in place, install a second continuous kraft-free batt between the stair frames to fill the opening.

WALLBOARD AND SPACKLE

Once your moisture barrier and insulation are in place, apply gypsum wallboard to the walls and ceiling of the wine cellar as a substrate for other finishes, an added layer of thermal mass and moisture protection, or as a final wall finish.

Gypsum wallboard comes in several different thicknesses and is finished with either a porous kraft-paper surface or with a moisture-proof surface; porous wallboard is gray or white, and moisture-proof wallboard is green—and is commonly referred to as "green board." Green board is used for wet-surface applications such as around and under a shower in a bathroom, the backsplash of a sink, a laundry room, or other applications where resistance to damp is vitally important. Consider green board if you expect higher than normal moisture inside your cellar, for instance in a damp basement.

Measuring, cutting, applying, and finishing wallboard require simple skills and tools to achieve good results. Applying wallboard to a cellar's walls can be completed in a single day; for small cellars you also may have time to tape the joints and apply joint compound. Always allow the joint compound to dry between applications, and sand the joint compound to achieve a smooth final finish.

If the walls of the cellar will be painted, it's best to apply joint compound to make a textured surface that hides imperfections. For wallcoverings, a smooth finish will be necessary; achieving a perfectly flat surface requires close attention to detail at each step of the process, as well as patience.

Follow these steps to install and finish wallboard in your cellar.

STEP 1

Measure the walls of your cellar, then transfer the length and width to panels of wallboard. Snap a chalkline or pencil-draw lines, using a steel straightedge, for reference while cutting. Most walls of standard height use full lengths of wallboard; the wallboard only requires cuts for its width.

STEP 4

Apply inside and outside metal corners as necessary. Tape and apply joint compound to each fastener location and all joints, filling indentations and making a smooth surface.

STEP 2

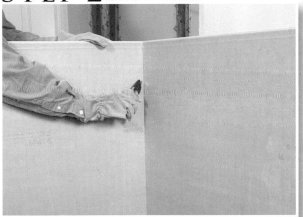

Score the paper-faced side of the wallboard using a utility knife and the straightedge at the marked line. Fold and break the wallboard from its back, and cut the backside of the panel along the fold's crease to divide the wallboard sheet into two sections. Repeat with other cuts as necessary.

STEP 3

If necessary, rasp or shave excess wallboard. Fit the panel tightly into place. Its thin, outer edge should face the next panel across the joint. Nail or screw the panel to the wall studs with wallboard screws; dimple nails and countersink screw fasteners slightly below the surface of the wallboard.

STEP 5

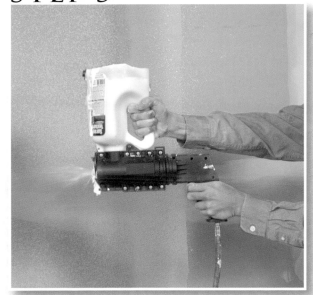

For so-called "knock-down" textured surfaces as seen here, apply joint compound with a pneumatic sprayer (available from rental yards). Allow it to set for 15–20 minutes.

STEP 6

Finish the surface texture using a broad steel blade. Omit multiple applications of tape, joint compound, and texture if wood paneling or another finish will cover the wallboard.

WAINSCOT PANELING

Wooden wainscoting is typically installed as individual slats in a process similar to that used for wood-strip flooring. It offers a pleasing alternative to painted wallboard as the backdrop to your wine racks, cabinets, countertops, and other finishes in the cellar.

Wainscoting used to require hours of tedious mortising and joining to achieve a quality installation; today, many kits with prefinished components are available. Most of them have routed grooves in the chair rails and baseboard moldings to hold the wainscot strips within them.

The secret to a good wainscot installation using kit strips is deciding where the first strip goes and getting it exactly vertical. Trial fit the pieces together to gain information about their measurements, and find the center point on the wall. You may need to rip the strips on each side to narrow them and fit the corner. The installation looks best when the two end strips are equal.

Prefinish all of the components, either by painting them on both sides and their ends, or by sealing them with a clear sealant. Install the baseboard molding first, then the wainscot strips, and finally the chair rail. Edge-nail through the tongue of each strip to hide the fasteners that hold it to the wall.

You'll need a pneumatic or mechanical brad gun to avoid drilling and applying finish nails; they are available from tool rental yards. Allow about four hours for an average-sized cellar.

Follow these steps for installing wood paneling.

STEP 1

Seal and paint or varnish all sides of the strips, chair rail moldings, and baseboard moldings and allow them to dry. Wine cellars are humid, and sealing the wood prevents it from absorbing moisture and warping.

STEP 4

Starting at a square, level corner, applying shims if needed. Rest a corner strip in the baseboard's routed groove, check that the strip is vertical, and fasten it in place by nailing through the corner edge and the tongue of the strip.

STEP 2

Square and apply the baseboard molding to the longest wall in the installation. If the wainscoting turns a corner, use a scrolling saw or jigsaw to cut a matching cove in the end of the baseboard molding set perpendicular to the first piece. Repeat the process at each subsequent corner. Avoid 45° miters at the corners.

STEP 3

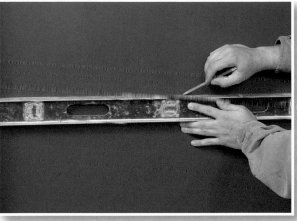

Use a carpenter's level to establish a horizontal guideline measuring from the baseboard molding's routed groove to the top of the wainscot strips. This guide will keep the installation square and level as you install the strips.

STEP 5

Apply subsequent wainscot strips, fitting them to the guideline and periodically checking that they are vertical. Nail through the tongue of each strip. The next strip's groove will fit over the nailed tongue, holding its edge in place.

STEP 6

When all of the strips have been applied, fit and fasten the chair rail in place with face-nailed brads. Set each brad with a nail set, and fill the indentions with plastic wood. When they are dry, touch up any marks with sealer or paint.

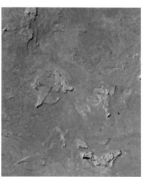

Top: Faux-painted sandstone blocks, shown here in detail and fully on the opposite page, are made of plaster.

Middle: Detail of sponged two-toned paint applied over wallboard with a textured surface. High points have been rubbed to remove some of their paint.

Bottom: Detail of a rag-rolled multitoned textured paint surface on smooth-finished wallboard creates the illusion of depth.

Paints and Varnishes

The last step of your wine cellar room's construction is to apply the wall finishes, specifically paint—for smooth or textured walls—or a stain or varnish on wainscot paneling. Apply a dark-colored paint to contrast with and highlight your wood wine racking systems, bins, and other equipment, features, and finishes.

Before applying any finish, mask off areas and edges that should avoid paint or stain. Special painter's tape, typically dark blue and available in many widths, effectively masks off areas and is easy to remove without leaving a residue. With each coat, including the prime or sealer coat, remove the tape once the paint or coating is dry to the touch and remask the area before applying the next coat.

Many paints are available. Choose a latex-based coating with additives that resist mold growth and peeling in moist or humid environments. Also consider coatings with low volumes of—or absent entirely of—volatile organic compounds (VOCs). Volatile chemicals evaporate as the paint dries, causing odor, at least, and perhaps respiratory problems and headaches. Paints with low VOCs and VOC-free formulas are generally as effective and durable as coatings with high VOCs.

To prepare for the finish coat of paint, first apply a primer coat to seal the drywall or wainscoting and keep it from absorbing the finish layer. Start with the walls and ceiling. Use canvas, oilcloth, or plastic drop cloths to protect the finished floor and other areas from spills and splatters.

Prepare for the finish coat by masking areas to be painted different colors such as trims or moldings. Use a two-inch (50-mm) or smaller brush to apply paint to the corners and the floor and ceiling junctions, making swaths about three or four inches (75 or 100 mm) wide. Finish the large areas of wall with a paint roller, using even, angled strokes to achieve full coverage. Plan to apply two or more coats of finish paint to achieve an even surface.

Clean brushes, trays, and rollers thoroughly between coats—or, using an old painter's trick, seal them in a plastic bag and store them in a refrigerator between coats. Consider disposable, inexpensive tray liners and roller brushes to save time. Also seal the lid of the paint can. Always store and dispose of leftover paint and partially full or empty paint cans following the paint can's label directions.

Select a stain color for wood wall finishes, such as paneling or trim, that complements your racking system. A redwood stain, for instance, makes your wine racking appear built-in, while a contrasting—often darker—stain color such as walnut helps the racks stand out from the wall. Test stain colors on scrap pieces of the wood you will finish to confirm it is the right color, and experiment to see how many coats you should apply to achieve the desired effect.

Apply stain following the manufacturer's label directions instructions, typically with a three inch (75-mm) brush using long strokes. Work in small areas. Allow the stain to penetrate for a few minutes before gently wiping away excess stain with a dry rag to emphasize the wood's grain. Allow the stain to dry to the touch before you apply another coat. Repeat the process until the wood is as dark as you desire.

Varnishes and clear coatings seal stained wood and preserve its color, especially in a wine cellar's humid environment. Apply at least two generous coats of a marine-rated varnish or polyurethane sealer to stained wood. Once the final coat is completely dry, or cured, use a piece of steel wool to lightly "sand" or smooth the surface to remove any imperfections. Deep-glazed varnished surfaces are best achieved with an airless paint sprayer.

Special Decorative Effects

Formed and textured plaster has been faux-painted to resemble the character of mortared limestone blocks. The surface of the "blocks" was sponged with three different tones of paint and then with clear glazes. The seams have faux "highlights" of light paint and "shadows" of darker paint. The effect is shown in detail on the opposite page.

Fine wine cellars often feature dramatic design details, including paneled ceilings, carved or molded columns, decorative and faux painting such as sponging, ragging, dragging, and other specialty treatments. Many wine cellars have mural paintings in alcoves and on walls. Decorative effects are an opportunity to showcase your creativity while inspiring others to enjoy visits to your cellar room and your wine collection. The best finishing details avoid overwhelming your wine collection for the sake of a dramatic detail.

Use a variety of racking systems, bins, and other storage solutions to add drama and interest to the cellar. Apply thick decorative moldings at the floor and where the walls join the ceiling to add depth and dimension to the space.

SPECIALIZED CELLAR EQUIPMENT

The heart of a home wine cellar is its refrigeration system. Choose cooling equipment that matches the size of your room, its thermal mass and insulation, and the size of your collection.

Custom wine cellars require their own dedicated equipment for refrigerating the space and maintaining its humidity. Depending on the cellar's location and capacity, you have a choice among self-contained, stand-alone units, split-refrigeration systems, and ducted air-handling refrigeration systems.

Self-contained, through-the-wall systems simply plug in or are hard-wired in the cellar. They are installed at the top of the cellar's wall and vented to an adjacent large area within the home. Because they can only cool air about 30°F (17°C) lower than the ambient temperature, you must install stand-alone units adjacent to spaces where the ambient temperature rarely exceeds 80°F (27°C) in order to keep the cellar within the desired temperature range.

In most installations, the backside of the unit mounts flush to the opposite side of the wall with its fan vents in the adjacent space. If this is the case and the unit will vent into another room, the adjacent space must be at least as large as the cellar, with good ventilation. Some units are noisy. Others have unsightly grills. Listen to the unit and judge its appearance before you make your choice.

Inside the cellar, the unit protrudes from the wall and into the room. Most models have thermostats located on top of their housings or attached by a cable to a movable probe; to allow the cool air to fall and hot air to rise, self-contained refrigeration units are placed in the racks as high on the wall as possible.

The chief advantage of stand-alone refrigeration units is their economical cost and simple electrical needs. For wine cellars smaller than 2,000 cubic feet (57 m³), they provide adequate cooling. Models are available with up to 8,000 BTUS—a measure of energy output. Determine the size you need by matching it to your cellar's cubic volume or the number of bottles it contains, depending on the information provided by the cooling equipment's manufacturer.

A split-refrigeration unit—or "split"—places a fan-and-condenser unit housing a heat exchanger outside the wine room

A self-contained, stand-alone wine refrigeration system has within its housing both an evaporator and a condenser unit that draw air from the room, cool it, and return it to the room. Moisture the air contains is caught in a condensation pan within the unit, where it evaporates back into the cellar.

and quietly dissipates hot air to a more distant and convenient location, usually outside the home. Though the evaporator—sometimes called the coil—remains on the inside wall of the cellar, noise is rarely an issue in the wine room. Splits operate with a standard, wall-mounted thermostat for added flexibility and control. They also outperform stand-alone units, are suitable for larger spaces, and can be more reliable than stand-alone units.

Split-refrigeration systems require professional installation and a larger budget than small, self-contained units. A mechanical contractor installs the various refrigerant lines and electrical conduits while the future cellar's walls are exposed, then returns once the room is nearly finished to install the unit, fill its coolant lines with refrigerant, and test the system.

An air-handling system is the most costly but also the best refrigeration option for large wine cellars. Like the central air conditioner serving a house, the system uses a series of vents and ductwork to force cool air into the room. All of its working parts are located outside the cellar, and so is the unit's noise. Vents inside the cellar— mounted high on the walls or ceiling   are easily hidden and finished.

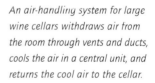

An air-handling system for large wine cellars withdraws air from the room through vents and ducts, cools the air in a central unit, and returns the cool air to the cellar.

As with split-refrigeration systems, air-handling systems have thermostats mounted inside on the cellar walls, and they also require professional installation.

Dedicated wine cellar refrigeration systems are designed to maintain a high level of humidity. Simply, the coil—or evaporator—is twice the size of the condenser (instead of the same size, as with a conventional refrigerator). As a result, the coil produces more air than the condenser can pull, and the moisture it contains remains in the cellar. Other refrigeration systems are designed with condensation recovery features.

Split-refrigeration systems have two parts: an evaporator coil with a fan inside the cellar, and an condenser unit located outside of the cellar and home.

Besides your cellar's refrigeration system, you may have to provide a separate humidifier—or, in rare cases, a dehumidifier—to ensure the cellar holds the recommended level of relative humidity. Either type of unit requires its own power source and plumbing to supply water or drain away condensation. Consult a mechanical contractor regarding available units sized for your wine room, installation costs, and operating instructions.

DO IT YOURSELF OR CONTRACT THE PROJECT?

Doing it all, doing part of it, or overseeing the work done by someone else are the three choices available to you as you plan your new wine cellar.

A typical homeowner's woodworking and home repair tools are ample for installing off-the-shelf wine racks, converting bookcases and cabinets to hold wine, or installing a freestanding wine chiller. Building a custom wine cellar or altering an existing area of your home requires more tools and greater expertise.

The decision you make to act as your own contractor or hire a professional is complicated and personal. Only you know your familiarity with construction techniques, your comfort level, and your skill levels. Your choice depends on your cellar project's scope. While many people with basic tools can install a freestanding wine chiller in an existing appliance bay or stand a wine rack in their family room, their numbers dwindle when you start replacing kitchen cabinets, running electrical cable, or building a full-blown wine cellar and butler's pantry in a basement.

Doing the work yourself will certainly help you economize. If you have the skills and are interested in doing most of the work yourself—and have several weeks of free time—make the decision to tackle the job yourself. Remember that a do-it-yourself job will take time away from family activities, vacations, and other pursuits. After you weigh the pros and cons, choose to do the work yourself or hire a professional.

Professional contractors, especially those who specialize in building wine cellars or converting existing space into conditioned wine rooms, offer years of expertise, skill gained on many projects, and management capabilities. They are adept at hiring and scheduling subcontractors for plumbing, electrical, and mechanical systems, following building codes and obtaining inspector approval to ensure safety, and many have a complete understanding of the nuances for creating a thermally efficient cellar in a variety of site conditions.

Many seasoned contractors, will also know reliable artisans who can create the stunning visual effects that you have seen in many of the photographs of wine cellars found in this book. They include artists, plasterers, decorative painters, wood carvers, and other specialists who make a wine room into a work of art.

If you decide to contract some or all of the work, select a contractor with a proven track record of projects similar to yours and a list of referrals to satisfied past clients. Ask for and check references before you commit to the job. Evaluate the contractor's financial stability by asking for bank references and contacting the contractor licensing board or the Better Business Bureau to check their records for complaints, legal actions, or settlements. Request a comprehensive contract that spells out every step of the project, and pay only as the work is completed to your satisfaction for progress and materials.

Even if you hire a contractor for your wine cellar project, your role will still be vitally important. In addition to the responsibility for hiring a reputable and trustworthy contractor, lead by example by adhering to deadlines, paying on time per the contract terms, and asking questions about the process employed and the materials used—and getting satisfactory input and answers—along the way. Make the outcome of the project a winner for both of you.

As a contractor that remodels space and builds custom cellars from scratch, the author's workshop has specialized jigs and streamlined production systems to make the custom components and racking that a wine cellar needs.

FINISHING TOUCHES FOR A CUSTOM WINE CELLAR

Change a refrigerated room into a wine cellar.

The final step before you can enjoy the benefits of your wine collection is putting the finishing touches on your wine cellar. With the basic shell completed, you'll now add features such as lighting fixtures, an insulated and weather-stripped door, and your chosen racking, bins, and shelves. The finishes you select, and how you apply them, depend somewhat on your circumstances: your choice of flooring, for instance, determines if you'll need a raised threshold and how you'll seal the bottom of the door. The refrigeration system you select governs some elements of the electrical system, such as the location of its outlets and hard-wired connections. Your wine room's size and its ceiling clearance dictate the lighting you'll install.

When your wine room's construction is finished, install its racks, fixtures, equipment, and finishes, turning it into a home for your wine collection.

In addition to its wine racks, your wine room may also include countertops, cabinets, and shelving that complete your vision for your cellar.

Finally, stocking your wine cellar requires careful control of the wine room's climate. When you move wine into a climate-controlled wine cellar for the first time, avoid "shocking" it by giving it a gradual adjustment.

THREE COMMON SITES FOR WINE CELLARS

A basement wine room, an understairs wine cellar, and a converted wine closet provide examples of frequently seen finishing elements for many wine storage projects.

A wine room in a basement corner invites your guests to sit and enjoy your company while sipping wine aged in your cellar.

Three of the most frequently converted spaces used for home wine cellars are old wardrobe or linen closets, newly constructed rooms in basement corners (above-ground rooms will also work), and an adapted understairs storage closet.

For the closets, the choice is simple: improve the utilization of existing space. In the case of the basement cellar, a wine room adds charm and function to an

area of the home that previously may have been ignored but which has ideal attributes for wine storage—great thermal mass, good insulation, passive cooling, and ample space for a large wine collection.

Consult the instructions in Chapter 5 to build the wine room itself. Here, you'll finish the electrical appointments of the room, then complete the space with racks, fixtures, furnishings, trims, flooring, and paint. You'll also apply the seals necessary for a tight fit around the heavily insulated door.

Many times, wine cellar racks are assembled within the space of the room —they simply are too large to fit through a standard doorway and assembly is done at the project site. Modular racks work best for these conditions [see Building Wooden Racks, page 54].

You'll also install your refrigeration system, connect it to an outlet or wire it to a junction box, and calibrate the thermostat to cool your room. Fine tuning the temperature and humidity settings may take several days from the time the unit is installed.

Let's look at each type of cellar site in turn on the following pages.

Left: An understairs cellar makes use of the high-ceiling under a stairs landing for a serving area, the sloped ceiling under the stairway for vertical racks, and the low-ceiling area as a place for diamond bins and bulk storage.

Right: Formerly a clothes closet stuffed with winter garb, this cellar now earns attention in an alcove off of a dining room.

WARDROBE CLOSET CELLAR

Builders put wardrobe and linen closets into spaces in homes left over after they divide the main rooms. Closets are nearly always wholly contained inside the conditioned living area of the home, and only rarely do they share one or more of their sides with exterior walls.

Although such closets are small, they are mighty when it comes to wine storage! Most are at least 24 inches (60 cm) deep, allowing for double-deep racks in the side facing the door, with single-deep racks to each side. A typical 2 × 4-foot (60 × 120-cm) wardrobe closet with an 8-foot (2.4-m)

ceiling can hold between 200 and 250 bottles of wine. A walk-in clothes closet, with its correspondingly larger capacity, can hold a more sizable collection of wine.

Take out the old closet hardware, and remove the interior wallboard from the closet. Install a vapor barrier [see Interior-Wall Vapor Barriers, page 114]. Insulate the closet [see Insulation, page 116]. Finally, install new wallboard and finish it [see Wallboard and Spackle, page 120, and Paints and Varnishes, page 124].

After the closet's interior has been prepared, follow the steps shown to install an insulated exterior door and complete a standard closet's adaptation into an air-conditioned wine room. You'll also need to weather-strip the door, as shown for the corner wine cellar project [see A Corner Wine Cellar, page 136]. Allow a weekend for finishing a prepared room into a new wine cellar.

STEP 1

Remove the existing interior door and its frame, and install a new prehung exterior door frame, door stops, jambs, and moldings. Remove the old closet hardware and shelves, then prepare the space with vapor barriers, insulation, and new wallboard as described in Chapter 5.

STEP 4

Assemble modular rack components, checking that they will fit through the doorway opening; if necessary, build the racks in sections and assemble them inside the closet.

STEP 2

Shim the prehung frame to plumb, and adjust the reveal between the door and the jamb until it is even. Cut and install shims as necessary. Seal the voids around the jamb with minimal-expanding foam. Apply the casing, stain or paint the door, and install its lockset hardware.

STEP 3

Turn off power to the room's circuit. Connect all electrical outlets to the wires previously run to their junction boxes. Install lighting fixtures and switches to their junction boxes. Restore the power. Install bulbs and test all switches, timers, and dimmers before proceeding.

STEP 5

Fasten the racking system to the studs in the closet's walls using wood screws. Attach baseboard moldings and crown moldings to finish the rack.

STEP 6

Install and adjust the refrigeration unit after plugging it in and testing its operation, reading completely and following exactly the manufacturer's directions.

A CORNER WINE CELLAR

The corner of an unfinished or finished basement is another great location for a wine cellar. Adding two walls in an exterior corner of a basement gives you a wine room suitable for most wine collections. The basement's subterranean location uses the passive cooling from the deep surrounding soil and the great thermal mass of its masonry walls, floor, and the surrounding soil to reduce the need for active refrigeration once the room has been brought to the proper wine storage temperature. You can also adapt a corner of an above-ground room using these same basic steps.

Once the room has been built, a vapor barrier applied, its walls insulated and finished, the space is ready for the features it needs to store and age wine.

You have many different design choices with respect to the finish materials you can use in a full-sized basement wine cellar. These finishes make the room ready to receive its racks, counters, and specialty lighting.

You can cover its slab concrete floor with ceramic, stone, or vinyl tiles, use sheet vinyl flooring as a finish, or paint or stain the basement's floor. As a preparation for painting, you can apply texture to the wallboard, or you can skip the texturing and install wood wainscoting, depending on your room's final design. You will also have practical matters to deal with including the installation of the weather stripping, threshold, and sweep for the insulated door, and setting the refrigeration equipment into its rough opening.

The steps required for this installation are seen at right and on the following pages. Allow three to five work days to finish your wine room—more if some materials must dry or cure before the next steps can be done.

STEP 1

After applying a sealer-prime coat, decorative painting of the walls can take place. Sponged, ragged, and dragged paint finishes that use progressively lighter or darker tones to achieve an aged look are popular choices for most wine cellars. A dark background looks best behind racks.

STEP 4

To seal the door, lay a bead of panel adhesive down the jamb under the area where the door stop will be installed, then nail the stop into the jamb.

STEP 2

Install the floor finish. Here, ceramic tile was applied with adhesive to the floor and is being grouted. It will extend to the door's threshold; the rest of the basement has carpeting outside the wine cellar. Other options for floor finishes are described in the introduction, opposite page.

STEP 3

Turn off the power to the room's circuits. Connect the wiring and install all receptacles and their covers. Install lighting fixtures and switches to their junction boxes. Restore the power. Install bulbs and test all switches, timers, and dimmers before proceeding.

STEP 5

Exterior door stops have a ⅛″ × ⅜″ routed groove to receive and hold weather stripping. Install it by pressing it into the groove. Check the operation of the seal as the door latches.

STEP 6

Install an exterior threshold, caulking beneath it. Attach a door sweep tight against the threshold. Turn off the lights in the cellar and look for light seeping through the seal.

A CORNER CELLAR (CONTINUED)

The basement corner wine cellar is nearly finished. Where the tile floor and carpet outside the room meet at the door, a metal threshold with a tight weather seal is installed to span the gap. The bottom of the door also receives a sweep that fits into the threshold's weather stripping. These two fixtures work together when the door closes to make a virtually airtight lock that helps keep warm drafts from entering the cellar.

Like the floor- and wall-finishing choices, there are many different kinds of electrical fixtures that are suited to a wine cellar. Try to avoid using recessed lighting that is built into the ceiling cavity between joists; it has large air gaps that permit warm air to enter the refrigerated room. A better choice is low-wattage rope lights—some are now available with light-emitting diodes that illuminate an area but remain nearly cold. Mount them behind the rails of the vertical racks or beneath soffits and behind crown moldings. You also can use low-wattage incandescent track lighting on a dimmer or 12-volt lights that emit little heat.

Hide lights in crevices, behind the racks to illuminate the bottles from behind, under counters, and at the junctions of the walls with the ceiling.

Last, you'll install your refrigeration system, if it is a small, plug-in unit. When the room is finished, run the unit for several hours and monitor the temperature within the room. It will take some time for all of the racks and fixtures to cool, so the unit will run nearly continuously at first, then intermittently at frequent intervals for several days.

Follow the steps shown to complete the wine room.

STEP 7

Assemble modular racks and fasten them through their back rails into the studs in the wall with wood screws. Check level and square before proceeding.

STEP 10

Install indirect rope lights under the inside edge of the rails, wiring its plug to a junction box or plugging it into a switch-controlled outlet.

STEP 8

Nail the racks' front rails in place, completing the straight sections. The horizontal rails should be spaced vertically so there is a rail for every six bottle rungs.

STEP 9

Install corner units of racking system as designed. Make sure that each ladder is parallel to the depth of a bottle. Attach bevel-cut baseboard and crown moldings.

STEP 11

Install track lighting and bulbs, and adjust their positions. Wire the track directly into a facing junction box. Spray expanding foam between the track and its junction box.

STEP 12

Mount the refrigeration system in its cutout, plug it into the outlet, and set the control thermostat panel into the faceplate. Test the unit, then mount its back panel.

AN UNDERSTAIRS CELLAR

An understairs location typically offers low ceiling clearances, tight quarters, and odd angles but may be a surprisingly roomy spot for a wine cellar. Often used as storage areas for seldom-used items, cleaning supplies, and clothing, they are good choices for conversions to wine rooms, especially if they are part of a basement.

If you are fortunate, a full-height stair landing will be part of the old closet. A landing has enough room beneath it to hold two walls with vertical racks, enough room for as many as 300 bottles of wine.

Some stairways are open underneath and will require wall construction to create the cellar. Structurally, stairways are self-supporting. They have wooden or metal stringers that span from their heads to their feet; you can usually remove framing beneath the girders as needed to enlarge or insulate the space as long as their supporting attachment points are kept intact. The adjacent walls to which they are frequently attached are another story; these are structural elements and always should be left intact—they also may be part of the support structure for the floor above.

You have to be creative when it comes to building racks and fitting shelves, counters, and lighting fixtures in an understairs cellar. Most stairs are about three to four feet (90 to 120 cm) wide, making their undersides narrow. To keep a corridor open, you may have to install single-bottle racking and bins or leave open areas for access. Use miniaturized light fixtures that can mount tightly against the wall near its apex.

An understairs wine cellar is cozy, but it can hold a surprisingly large quantity of wine—up to 1,000 bottles under some longer stairways. The stair risers and treads also have extra space for added insulation.

Finishing an understairs cellar will require about two days to complete, following the steps shown.

STEP 1

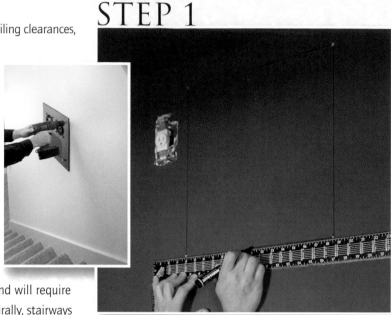

Install blocking in the wall frame for the refrigeration unit when the walls are constructed. After painting, open the installation area and mount the unit after reading completely and following the manufacturer's directions.

STEP 4

Install a 12-volt lighting transformer on the wall and plug it into an outlet. Connect the lead wires and install track wires using wallboard anchors. Install fixtures on the track.

STEP 2

Assemble and install individual-bottle vertical racks, bringing partially assembled modules into the cellar. Tailor racks to the sloped ceiling, and attach their back rails to the studs in the wall using wood screws.

STEP 3

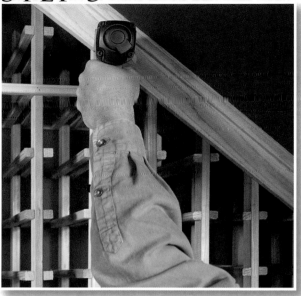

Attach the racks' front rails after the back. Finish the rack by installing crown molding to cover the ceiling junction, then install the baseboard molding at the floor. The rack should be totally stable when installation is complete.

STEP 5

Install diamond bins for bulk storage in low-ceiling areas of the understairs cellar, leaving access space between the bins and the vertical racks. Install countertops.

STEP 6

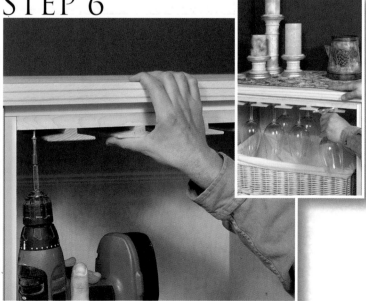

Install cabinets and counters. Install stemware hangers and fit baskets into open shelving. Hang stemware from hangers and fill the baskets with linens.

BASEMENT INSTALLATIONS

Some tips and suggestions for finishing a basement wine room with an adjacent tasting room for serving your guests.

Finish a custom-built or prefabricated basement wine room the same way as you would above-grade cellars or adapted spaces—with a few notable differences.

The concrete slab floor of the cellar limits your choice of floor finishes. Standard solid wood plank or strip flooring, for instance, is impossible to fasten directly to a concrete substrate. While engineered wood and laminate floors designed to replicate solid wood can be installed over moisture barrier–protected concrete and allowed to "float" without any fastening system, the humid conditions of the cellar might cause the floor to buckle after installation—in turn threatening the integrity of the door seal.

Ceramic tile is a more practical option, but the uneven surface it creates requires you to install a raised threshold at the door opening to achieve an effective seal [see A Corner Wine Cellar, page 136]. Vinyl sheet flooring, available in a variety of patterns and textures that replicate slate, wood, and other finishes, is another cost-effective, durable, and easy-to-install floor finish for basement wine cellars.

Consider the simple option of finishing the concrete slab itself with paint or epoxy coatings, perhaps with a non-skid finish. Simple coatings may also help level the floor and create an even surface. Finished concrete leaves exposed the additional thermal mass of the concrete in a basement wine cellar, performs well in the room's humid conditions, provides a stable base for racking and other finishes, and most closely resembles the wine cellars you might visit at a winery.

A basement cellar often has enough space within it to accommodate supplemental and short-term storage of fruit and vegetables, cut flowers, and other items that benefit from storage in the room's cool, humid climate. If you envision using the wine room to keep those and other belongings, design and provide separate, out-of-the-way areas with storage cabinets and closets in the wine cellar for them.

Opposite page: An alcove in a descending staircase is a showcase for decorative items in a vintner's theme. It helps bridge the change between the living area above and the wine cellar beneath.

Lighting considerations in a basement cellar may also be slightly different from those found in an above-grade location. This is especially true if the rest of the basement is left unfinished. Keep high-voltage and -wattage lighting to a minimum; provide low-level general lighting. Use track light or indirect lighting systems that allow you to add fixtures as needed,

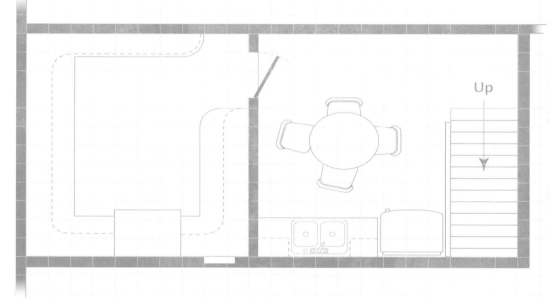

and direct the beams from fixtures to showcase areas or special racking systems. Under-counter lights also may be used to provide adequate light for working on a counter or illuminating the room. Control all lighting with dimmers or even adjustable timers, and remember that lighting use should be kept to a minimum.

As with any climate-controlled wine storage area, take care to acclimate your wine collection to your cellar's environment, especially if you move wine from a room-temperature location into the cool, humid confines of a basement wine room. Set the initial temperature near that of the wine's current environment, e.g., 68°F (20°C), then lower it 1° to 2°F (0.6°–1.1°C) every other day. Allow the bottles to adjust slowly until you eventually reach your desired temperature setting within the recommended range.

A full-height basement measuring 12' × 22' (3.7 × 6.7 m) has ample space for both an 850-bottle wine room and an entertaining area with a sink, a refrigerator, and seating. This is the best arrangement for your wine; it is kept in the ideal temperatures and humidities for aging, while guests are comfortable in the heated room next door. Three-dimensional drawings that illustrate this basement wine cellar and entertaining area are found on pages 109 and 111.

NEW CONSTRUCTION ABOVE GROUND

A separate structure for wine is the dream of every wine connoisseur. If you are building a new home, plan to include one as part of its design.

What could be more enjoyable than sitting on this patio on a warm summer evening and enjoying a fine red wine drawn from your personal stock? Just venture down the stairs and through the arched door to explore the bottles gathering age and greatness within its walls.

More so than an adapted closet or converted basement of an existing home, the opportunity to design and build a custom wine cellar within the floor plan of a newly constructed home or as a stand-alone structure affords you creative flexibility in terms of convenience, location, system features, capacity, layout options, finishes, materials, and methods of construction.

If you have a passion for wine and envision a growing collection, consider the value of a dedicated wine room adjacent to your kitchen or dining/living areas or to serve as part of an outdoor entertainment space, secondary kitchen, or home theater. Design your floor plan to take full advantage of your wine cellar.

A dedicated wine room built as part of your new house adds resale value equal to or exceeding its actual cost. Increasingly, luxury home buyers—whether in the market for a new or existing house—look for in-home amenities. Wine rooms are usually near the top of their wish lists, especially custom cellars in a convenient, above-ground location adjacent to the main structure. The ability to properly store wine and entertain your guests by hosting tastings and dinner parties near your cellar extends its value to you and your family, and to the prospective future buyers of your home.

An above-ground location also affords the opportunity to showcase your wine collection with view windows in the doorway or the walls of the cellar. Insulated and deep-tinted glass is essential to limit thermal transfer and excessive light into the cellar, but include some glazed panels to allow guests and visitors to admire your racking and wine without entering the cellar itself. Add other niches and alcoves to add architectural interest but keep light to a minimum.

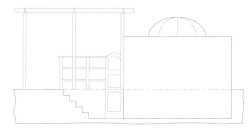

A stand-alone wine cellar, based on the wine room seen on the opposite page, features an adjacent patio beneath a shade cover for entertaining. Its walls are partially sunk into the surrounding soil. This adds thermal mass and reduces the expense of its split-refrigeration system. When you enter the cellar, its cloisterlike coiffed-arch ceiling creates the illusion of the open sky above, with ranks of wine racks below. The cellar's dimensions are 8' × 10' (2.4 × 3 m), and it holds 1,200 bottles.

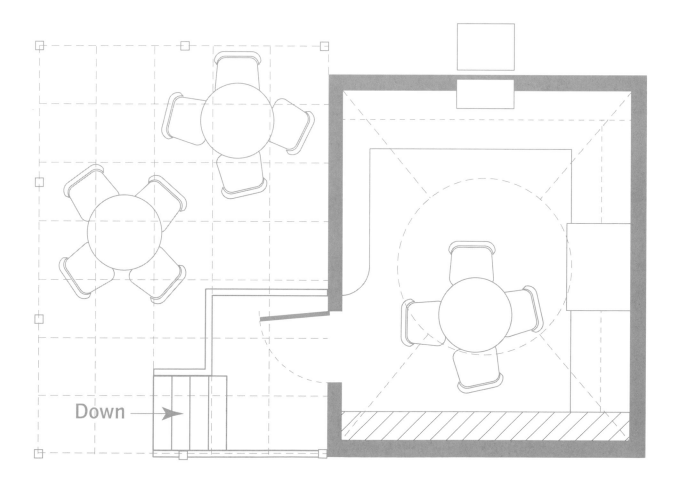

Down →

Tips for Dedicated Construction

An above-ground wine room built during the construction of a new home allows you to select and use the ideal location, materials, cooling systems, and building methods to achieve optimum wine room conditions. Use 2 × 6 wall framing to achieve higher R-values in the insulation of your wine room's wall and ceiling cavities; design for high or curved ceilings able to hide indirect lighting in its niches or worthy of a special decorative paint finish; and locate the space away from exterior walls to limit solar heat gain and allow for a quiet, split air-handling refrigeration system. Design for the weight of your wine and build your cellar within the engineered loads of a raised floor system. It's far easier to do as you build than as a retrofit after the home is finished.

Room Requirements. Choose the best cooling and humidifying systems for your wine collection, the ideal racking and other storage options for your bottles and cases, and the most attractive and effective lighting fixtures—in fact, make inspired choices for each element key to a wine room. Design and build a cellar that meets your vision and passion for wine, and include areas outside of the cellar for decanting and small-group tastings.

Layout Options. A custom wine room designed in the context of a new home also enables you to tightly pack racking systems and other storage fixtures, achieving maximum density and storage volume. In most cases, vertical, individual bottle racking is the best choice for along cellar walls, while peninsulas and islands of freestanding racks and shelves serve varietals, showcase special labels, or segregate mature wines.

Illuminated cases for stemware keeps the glasses clean and groups various varietal shapes together. A stemware case is a useful addition to a butler's pantry or tasting area outside the main wine cellar.

The wine cellar seen here is built off of the living room of the home, and it is accessed by passing through the informal tasting room, with its distinctive, wrought-iron vine-covered windows and door. It also can be seen on page 131.

In addition to permanent racks fastened to walls or built into niches and alcoves, consider movable storage that allows you to customize the room's layout and accommodate the new directions your collection may take.

Construction Steps. Building a custom wine cellar starts with proper planning and design, followed by a step-by-step through the project's rough carpentry and its prefinishing and finishing phases. In this case, the cellar is another element in the larger project of a new home's construction, and its steps will likely follow the overall building schedule. Its walls will go up with the other walls of the house; the insulation and moisture barriers will be installed at the same time as other fiberglass-batt and rigid-foam insulation panels; and the electrical and mechanical systems, including vents and ductwork, will be included in the work as the various contractors install similar systems to serve the rest of the house. As a result, construction of the room may take longer—at least as long as the rest of the house—than would be the case for remodeling a space in an existing house. On the other hand, it will be completed and ready for you to stock when the rest of the home is finished and you move into your new house.

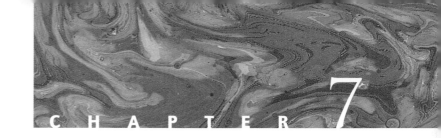

ACQUIRING, MANAGING, AND ENJOYING WINE

A wine collector's reward is the enjoyment of drinking it.

Creating wine storage—especially a custom-built cellar—underscores your enthusiasm for wine. As your knowledge grows, you'll earn a greater appreciation for wine culture and be tempted to visit wineries and host tasting parties.

A wine cellar affords you opportunities to acquire, manage, and enjoy wine. Expand your wine collecting experience beyond retail wine shops—visit wineries and participate in auctions.

Managing a cellar means making the right choices as you add wines to your collection, store it for proper lengths of time, and present it to your guests.

As your collection grows and your tastes broaden, you may wish to keep records of the wine in your cellar and track wine labels using manual or electronic means.

Your appreciation of fine wine means you'll care for the bottles in your collection. You'll learn how long to store wine to age it properly and discover the differences between grape varietals.

You'll also gain experience in opening and decanting wine, hosting tasting parties, and appreciating the intimate relationship between wine and food. As your knowledge grows, friends and family will trust your recommendations—and they'll count on you to bring the right wine when you get together.

THE WINE MARKET

Whether you acquire wine at the local grocery or in a wine auction, there are satisfying wines available for immediate drinking, and there are truly fine wines suited to aging.

The wine distribution system consists of wineries and wholesalers (including distributors, shippers, and importers), as well as retail outlets or government liquor stores. They work together to bring you both production and quality wine. Wine auctions, both live and online, also provide an active aftermarket for collectors and enthusiasts.

Most mass-market wines are produced for immediate consumption or, at best, are destined to last for a few years beyond their vintage dates. Wineries blend and wholesalers release these young wines while they are appropriately affordable—given their immaturity—to spur sales and quickly recoup their investments. For the finer reds, however, a winery may hold and release a vintage

Wine shops are retailers with a specialized knowledge about wines and an extensive inventory. For novice collectors, the staff of a wine store can aid your explorations of new grapes and wineries.

in smaller lots over a span of time. They believe that scarcity and demand will drive up the value of the wine—as well as their profits.

Remember, always, that price is among the least reliable gauge of a wine's quality; what really matters is whether you like its taste and other attributes. The best wines in your collection, in fact, could be among the most affordable.

Most wineries have tasting rooms and retail wine shops on their premises. Often they are included as the last stop on a winery's tour, a place where tastings are offered and wine is sold directly to the public. A certain volume of a winery's output is dedicated to these operations, but most wineries sell the bulk of their annual production to wholesalers that, in turn, sell small lots to local retailers.

Walk into a wine shop or the wine section of your local market and you'll see just a tiny fraction of the many thousands of labels and varietals of wine.

As you first start to collect wine and begin to gain knowledge about it, look for a local wine shop with a dedicated wine steward or in-house staff expert able to suggest varieties and vintages, help you choose food and wine pairings, and perhaps even host a tasting for you and your friends as you develop favorites.

Wine merchants will be up-to-date on wine reviews, and also will be able to offer their personal opinions about new releases. They will keep healthy stocks of both popular labels and personal favorites, and will intimately know the state of local, national, and international wine markets.

A dedicated wine shop is also more likely to give proper care to the wine in its charge than is a grocery or liquor outlet, storing bottles horizontally in racks or in cases away from light and heat, using a single upright bottle for display.

In fact, the display bottle may be just that. As you select a particular label, insist on receiving a bottle that has been properly stored—with at least a moist cork, if storage at an ideal temperature is impossible.

Buy bottles of several different comparable wines and conduct a tasting before you commit to a volume purchase. Retailers often offer discounts when you're

In wine country, you'll find that tastings have become big business. Tour operators guide thousands of tasters through the tasting rooms of major wineries—those with only a casual interest as well as serious buyers of fine wines. You can also visit wineries on your own. Wineries are found in nearly every area of the country.

willing to purchase a case or more of either a mix of several labels or a single wine variety. Once you find a favorite, be sure your retailer has access to and can supply larger quantities. It's always disappointing to discover exciting wines only to find out that their availabilities are limited.

Most distributors, on the other hand, primarily serve retailers rather than individual collectors, while wineries will sell consumers either individual bottles or case quantities —providing you can travel to the winery and pick it up. Some wineries will also ship wine to your home, if your state is one in which the governmental liquor authority has authorized them to do so.

More likely, you'll want to tour winery facilities clustered in one of the ever more common wine-producing regions. Winery tours give insights into the vintner's wine-making process, demonstrate the fermentation and aging stages, and usually include tastings of each winery's current vintages. It's easy to acquire wine at most wineries.

Buying direct from a winery and transporting it yourself assures that the wine has received proper care at all times and will age without spoilage in your cellar; wines that travel from producer to wholesaler and beyond to the retail shelf have likely suffered temperature swings, exposure to light, heat, and vibration, any or all of which could have damaged them.

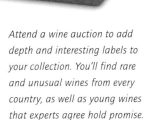

Attend a wine auction to add depth and interesting labels to your collection. You'll find rare and unusual wines from every country, as well as young wines that experts agree hold promise.

Each winery, of course, sells only its own product—a good reason to spend several days touring a near or distant wine country to visit a number of facilities. Extended tastings enable you to select wines you like for your cellar and enrich your overall knowledge of wine. The differences that mark bottlings of the same grape varietals and vintages in wineries just a few miles apart can be remarkable.

Wine auctions are another source of wine for your collection. They have become a prized source of sought-after labels, aged wines, and reserve bottlings purchased as much for their prestige as for their perceived quality. (It's a fact that the quality of some very old and pricey wines included in auctions may be reduced to little more than vinegar, but still they retain a cachet among collectors and connoisseurs.) In late 2003, a case of Chateau Lafleur 1961 sold for US$73,438, while a mere six bottles from the famous 1945 vintage of Chateau Mouton-Rothschild garnered US$70,500, both records. Such rare and antique wines are occasionally—though rarely—drinkable.

Live wine auctions worldwide account for nearly $100 million in annual wine sales, with online auction sales contributing more than $16 million[1] of that amount—figures that benefited from 1997 U.S. legislation legalizing wine auctions and the advent of Internet auctions—before that date, the authorities permitted only wine auctions in which the proceeds went to charities.

While auction houses in New York and London dominate the global market, a bit of research and reading of wine publications will reveal other wine auctions closer to you. Online auctions, meanwhile, especially those on dedicated wine-bid websites, allow you to search for wine by a variety of parameters, including labels, price, vintage, and grape varietal—in the comfort of your own home and at your leisure.

Online wine auctions draw a wide spectrum of buyers and increase the variety found in lots and labels, but they miss the mark when it comes to replicating the experience of attending a live auction in person, an opportunity that you should enjoy. Prepare before attending: comb auction catalogs and cross-reference lots that interest you, plan for purchases, and set a maximum budget before you enter the facility to avoid catching auction fever and overpaying for a lot.

Once at the auction, take it slow. Watch other bidders, note their interaction with the auctioneer, and study the pace and cadence of the bidding. Raise your paddle to make a bid, and acknowledge the auctioneer with a nod or wave. The best times to score bargains are early in the auction, during lulls in the bidding, and when identical or multiple lots of the same wine come on the block. Above all else, soak up the atmosphere and enjoy the culture and the experience.

Visit wine auction websites to satisfy your curiosity and find wines worth trying. These virtual auctions bring together sellers and buyers of fine wines.

[1] 2003 sales, according to *Wine Spectator* magazine.

INVENTORY CONTROL

Cellar inventories include records about each bottle and the lots stored in its racks, bins, and shelves. A growing collection demands proper documentation.

Wine cellar software tracks each bottle of your collection electronically, noting the date you acquired it, its cost, the early promise you noted at first tasting, and its progressive development at each subsequent tasting.

Any wine collection—especially one stored in a cellar with hundreds of bottles in various stages of aging—deserves attention to its condition and history. There are many different ways to approach record-keeping about your wine collection, ranging from simple notes on the bottle labels and tags that hang from their necks to elaborate computer database storage systems.

Start with the practical: use storage bins or actual winery cases to keep bottles from the same label and vintage together, and group varietals in your wine racking system for easier reference and access. Vertical racks for individual bottles are frequently constructed with six bays above and below a slant shelf, allowing you to store either a full or a half-case of wine in a single vertical column. Other cellar systems have modules that cellar six bottles per row, giving you a similar capacity.

Consider a wine cellar book to track your collection's acquisitions, your tasting experiences, and your inventory rotation. A wine cellar book can be as detailed as you want. It can simply list each bottle or case by its label, vintage, and date of purchase, or it can include notes about the source winery, its region, and terroir—the soil on which it was grown—plus notes on why you selected the wine, the various dates you've opened and tasted it, whether it is best decanted or poured directly from the bottle, its precise cellar location, suggestions for food combinations that you've tried and enjoyed with its flavor, and any other relevant observations you may want to make about it. Of course, the book may simply be a keepsake that allows you to provide information to pass along to your guests, heirs, or subsequent owners. As your interest, passion, and collection grows, the book will also track your progress as a wine lover.

Wine cellar books are especially handy and relevant if you plan eventually to sell some of your wine collection at an auction. The more detail you can provide about a wine's history and its care for the auction catalog, the more likely you'll foster attentive bidding and fetch a higher price.

In addition to a wine book, consider labeling your bins, shelves, and racking to identify wines and help you find bottles as you search the cellar for the ideal label. Winery cases are usually branded with the insignia and name of the winery, but you can add information such as the grape varietal and vintage year for even better reference; include a tally that tells you how many bottles remain.

Given the cool, humid conditions of a wine room, affix plastic labels or laminated paper labels to your storage units and cases. Plastic will protect the labels from moisture, mold, and soiling. Check the labels periodically and update them as you remove and consolidate bottles in your collection.

Another alternative to record keeping is wine collecting software. Just as online auctions have expanded the wine market, software programs for personal computers enable you to keep track of your wine collection electronically. Electronic inventory control, like a wine cellar book, provides a detailed and current history of your collection. Depending on your attention to regular back-ups of its data, it can also be more secure than its paper counterpart, and it has the great benefit of allowing quick electronic searches of the wine attributes you are seeking.

Several options exist when it comes to software. Choose from a dedicated wine inventory software program, a general database program, or even a simple spreadsheet program that can maintain the basic information needed for wine inventory management. You can customize or add notes and other details to all these types of software systems.

Bottleneck tags are a low-tech solution for noting important information about the wines in your collection. Both self-adhesive and simple die-cut hanger tags are popular with wine enthusiasts.

MAINTAINING YOUR CELLAR

Most of the time, your bottles will rest quietly in your cellar's or wine appliance's solitude, darkness, and silence. Here are some tips to help you care for your wine during storage.

A step stool is useful when you must place or withdraw wine from the upper bins and rack bays of a high-ceilinged cellar. Choose one that is sturdy and made of materials that will endure in the humidity of a cellar.

In addition to keeping track of your collection and monitoring its use, regularly inspect and maintain the conditions of your cellar or storage area to ensure that the wine ages properly under the optimum conditions that will enhance its flavor and value.

While you may be tempted to replicate the romance or dusty, musty environment of a winery's cellars or caves, the wine bottles and cases in your in-home cellar—as well as your bins, shelves, and racking—will maintain their structural integrity and finishes longer with regular care and constant temperature and humidity conditions.

Inspect regularly for mold and mildew growth, and periodically check and perform all the necessary maintenance of your cooling system to keep its operation reliable. Refrigeration systems should be professionally serviced at least once a year.

Finally, keep an eye on your racking systems and storage bins. Quality fixtures, built with the highest-grade wood, should last many years. Keep them in good repair and avoid overloading them.

Cleaning and Caring

As discussed earlier, the cool, humid conditions of a temperature-controlled wine cellar may lead to minor moisture problems ranging from mold and mildew growth to the deterioration of labels, wooden cases, and racks.

If you suspect moisture problems in your cellar, consider reducing its relative humidity to the lower end of the recommended range of 50 to 75 percent. Blot affected labels and fixtures such as racking or wine cases with lukewarm, soapy water to which a few drops of household bleach have been added. Allow the solution to stand for a few minutes, then rinse the bottles thoroughly and let them air dry within the cellar. Throughout the process, avoid allowing moisture from reaching the closure or cork.

Preserve wine bottle labels in a too-humid cellar by wrapping them in clear plastic or replacing deteriorated ones with self-made labels that identify the winery, grape varietal, vintage year, and other relevant facts from the original labels.

Problems can also occur when the relative humidity within a wine storage area is too low, including staining from dry, leaky corks. This is common in many ambient-temperature wine racks. Endeavor to keep the relative humidity within the recommended range to avoid these problems, using trays containing water, wet sponges, or a humidifier to add moisture to the storage area's air.

A sealed wine room seldom experiences problems with dust. Dust buildup in your cellar may appear romantic; but it also leads to deteriorating labels, and it can make it difficult to locate the desired bottles for a tasting or dinner party. If dust should accumulate, care for your wine with periodic dusting with a soft brush as you would any fine collectible, use a hand vacuum with a probe, and periodically replace the filters of your cooling system.

In addition to these steps, keep the areas around your wine racks, bins, and shelves free of clutter, eliminate items that might emit odors that could contaminate the wine, and promptly repair any damage or wear-related gaps in the cellar's door, its weather-stripping, or its threshold sweep.

As wines in your cellar age and mature, consider standing them upright for a few days before drinking to concentrate their sediment. Short periods of storage upright in a humid cellar is appropriate for wines such as sparkling wines, ports, and sherries. Wipe the bottles down and rap their bottoms sharply on a padded cellar counter as you place them. This dislodges sediment that will fall slowly to settle on the bottle's bottom.

SUGGESTIONS FOR STORAGE

Proper aging of fine wines results from cellar temperatures being maintained in a specific, narrow range over periods of time that vary with the grape varietals.

This red wine was cellared in mud within a cave for aging at its winery. The stains and clinging clay it bears are marks of its distinctive provenance.

Because most wineries use sterile microfiltration during the wine-making process to remove live yeast and mold cells, wine spoilage is kept to a minimum —unless the wine oxidizes due to prolonged exposure to varying temperatures, dry air conditions, excessive light, or contaminating odors. Wine that has received proper care and handling from the winery to your cellar seldom produces an "off" bottle.

While it's true that a properly aged wine may release a slight odor upon opening, the bottle-trapped odors resulting from anaerobic oxidation quickly dissipate in the open air, leaving the mature wine's full bouquet intact. Any offensive odors that persist for longer than a minute or two probably indicate an oxidized wine that should be discarded, as would discoloration, cloudiness, and a flat, metallic taste.

Proper storage of wine addresses such problems. Lay corked bottles so that their corks are kept moist by the wine inside. Maintain a constant temperature between 55° and 65°F (13° and 18°C), with relative humidity between 50 and 75 percent. Avoid exposure to excessive light, heat, vibration, and rough handling.

Aging and Serving Wine

A wine's maturation process begins in the vineyard fields as the grapes ripen and continues through fermentation; cask, barrel, or vat aging at the winery; bottling; and travel within the wine market to your cellar.

Though many of today's fine wines are vinified to mature faster than past vintages, most of them benefit from proper cellaring for at least a year or two, and fine red wines should be aged even longer. Storage at temperatures of 50°F (10°C) or lower allows you to nearly stop the aging process and hold a particularly enjoyable wine for many years.

A wine room or quality wine appliance affords you opportunities to enjoy wine aged to perfection and track its progress toward that goal. The chart at right gives guidelines for aging various grape varietals stored in full bottles under ideal cellar conditions [see Wine Aging Recommendations Chart, at right].

Wine Aging Recommendations

Varietal	Years of Aging to Peak (from Vintage Date)
Reds	
Barolo	5–10
Cabernet Sauvignon	5–15
Chianti	1–6
Médoc	5–20
Merlot	3–8
Petit Syrah/Shiraz	2–10
Pinot Noir	1–5
Zinfandel	2–5
Whites	
Chardonnay	1–5
Château Grillet (Rhône)	1–5
Pinot Grigio	1–2
Rhône	3–10
Riesling	1–5
Sauvignon Blanc	2–5
Others	
Blush/Rosé	0–1
Champagne	1–5
Madeira/Sherry	up to 60
Port	15–20 (typical[1])

[1] Some ports continue improving for up to 50 years

Wine Serving Temperature Recommendations

Varietal	Serving Temperature	Varietal	Serving Temperature
Reds		**Whites**	
Barbera	54°–57°F (12°–14°C)	Chardonnay	50°–55°F (10°–13°C)
Barolo	60°–63°F (16°–17°C)	Burgundy, White	54°–57°F (12°–14°C)
Beaujolais Nouveau	48°–52°F (9°–11°C)	Pinot Grigio	48°–52°F (9°–11°C)
Bordeaux	61°–64°F (16°–18°C)	Rhône	50°–54°F (10°–12°C)
Burgundy	58°–63°F (14°–17°C)	Riesling	43°–48°F (6°–9°C)
Cabernet Sauvignon	61°–64°F (16°–18°C)	Sauvignon Blanc	48°–52°F (9°–11°C)
Chianti	57°–61°F (14°–16°C)		
Merlot	57°–61°F (14°–16°C)	**Others**	
Petit Syrah/Shiraz	61°–64°F (16°–18°C)	Blush/Rosé	45°–50°F (7°–10°C)
Pinot Noir	57°–64°F (14°–18°C)	Champagne	46°–51°F (8°–11°C)
Rhône, Red	58°–63°F (14°–17°C)	Madeira/Sherry	48°–52°F (9°–11°C)
Zinfandel	61°–64°F (16°–18°C)	Port	61°–64°F (16°–18°C)

THE TASTING EXPERIENCE

Follow the steps a professional sommelier takes to select, open, decant, and taste wine. Learn the basics of how foods are paired with wines.

The time has come to open your wine and share it with friends and family. As with planning your wine room and stocking and storing your collection, this stage of the process offers common-sense guidelines to enhance your experience.

Following the preferred methods for opening and decanting wine means that you will fully enjoy the wine you've spent years aging [see Opening Wines, page 162, and Decanting, page 164).

When you open a bottle of wine, it releases gases held in the ullage and exposes the liquid to fresh air. The wine rapidly absorbs oxygen, changing the wine's aroma and flavor as you uncork, pour, smell, and taste it in a process referred to as rapid maturation. Some fine wines literally bloom under the influence of fresh air, releasing their delicious bouquet and flavor trapped in the must when the grapes were crushed. Take the time to embrace these changes as they occur, allowing a well-aged wine to reveal its full spectrum as you enjoy it.

Jorge Tinoco, sommelier for Wente Vineyards restaurant and visitor center in the historic Livermore Valley wine region of northern California, draws a bottle from the restaurant's extensive cellar which holds wines from around the country and the world. Wente has been producing fine wines since 1883.

Practiced at its highest level, wine tasting is an adventure rich in ceremony. Professional tasters who judge a current year's releases follow a strict script to ensure they get an accurate taste. You can adopt some or all of their procedures, or you can be as casual as you wish. Home tasting parties, for instance, are usually far less formal than serious tastings held by wine buyers. Even so, these events serve to broaden your experience with wine, giving you perspectives outside the realm of your previous experiences.

Use wine tastings as an opportunity to try new grape varietals, compare your favorite wines to untried labels, vintages, and sources, and share your cellar and collection—and joy of wine—with others. Rely on similar tasting methods to those followed by the pros to gain the most benefit from an informal tasting [see The Tasting Ritual, page 166].

Regardless of your purpose, limit the number of wines you taste at any given time and avoid spicy and heavily flavored foods—or other strong aromas, including cut flowers, perfumes, colognes, coffee, and tobacco—that influence your taste and smell. It's popular to offer neutral, salt-free crackers or breads between each bottle to help cleanse your palate.

Always use clean glasses free of soap residue when tasting wine. Specific glasses exist for nearly every popular type of wine; choose one with a large bowl, a moderately wide opening, and a sufficiently tall stem that permits your entire hand to hold it [see Glassware and Its Storage, page 24].

In general, professional tasters recommend organizing your samples in a progression from dry—or tart—whites to dry reds, and dry wines to sweet, light- to heavy-bodied, and young vintages before aged wines.

As you broaden your wine collecting and tasting experience and you gain knowledge, you'll develop your own nuances to these rituals; adapt them to suit the occasion and learn how to truly enjoy wine.

Top row: Corkscrews come in many fascinating designs. Antique corkscrews are highly collectible for wine enthusiasts.

Above: Unusual and fascinating paraphernalia abound in the world of wine. Here, you see a wine thermometer that was used to check the heat of fermentation in the crushed grape must.

OPENING WINES

On its face, it may seem intuitive, but presenting and opening a corked bottle of wine requires concentration and skill. Attention to detail will enhance enjoyment of the wine by you and your guests.

Presentation

The first phase of the opening is presentation of the bottle of wine. Presenting consists of drawing your guests' attention to four aspects of the wine:

- its vintage and country of origin
- the producing winery
- the name of the wine or its grape varietal
- the vineyard, terroir, and designation (appellation, status of reserve, or other special notice)

If you have tasted the wine in the past, the presentation is a good time to provide its tasting history and any observations you may have about its quality, improvement with age, expectations for the future, or potential for use with various foods.

Opening the Wine

The second phase is opening the wine. In preparation for opening, aged reds with sediment may be stood upright in your cellar for a period ranging from a few days to a few weeks. This will concentrate the sediment at the base of the bottle. If you plan to decant the wine, this step can be skipped. Careful opening and pouring will leave most of the sediment on the side of the bottle.

Follow the steps shown to ensure a clean extraction of the cork from the bottle.

STEP 1

Slowly bring the bottle to the preferred serving temperature over a period of 24 to 48 hours; either transfer it to a self-contained wine appliance with one zone kept at the desired temperature, allow it to warm slightly in a cool room, or set it within a terra-cotta wine chiller that has been soaked in water—or try serving wine, reds and whites, at cellar temperature; some wines may surprise you as they change character.

STEP 4

Insert the corkscrew's spiral tip into the center of the cork and turn the corkscrew until it penetrates about two-thirds of the cork. Gently extract the cork from the bottle.

STEP 2

Present the bottle with its label toward the taster [see directions for presentation in the introduction at left]. From the time it is presented until the bottle has been opened, sampled, and poured for guests, the bottle should remain within the taster's sight.

STEP 3

Carefully cut and remove the foil covering over the cork, using the point of a knife, the corkscrew's tip, or a foil cutter to score it near the lip of the bottle. Wipe the cork, lip, and neck with a clean, damp towel, removing any cork particles or clinging residue.

STEP 5

Remove the cork from the corkscrew. Note whether the cork is moist or dry. Provide it for the taster's visual inspection or to keep as a memento.

STEP 6

Wipe the top of the bottle, then inside its lip to remove any cork bits or wine residue. You can pour the open bottle of wine immediately, decant it, or allow it to breathe—stand for a time to absorb oxygen from the air.

DECANTING

Decanting transfers wine from its bottle to another container, removes sediment, and allows oxygen from the air to enter the wine before serving. You can also decant wine to blend several bottles of the same label, varietal, and vintage when you need larger volumes to serve or taste, or when you wish to combine the contents of two open bottles to be refilled and recorked as one.

Decanters come in many different sizes and shapes. Most have narrow top openings and flared sides that lead to a wide base. The decanter's shape helps the wine flow down the glass sides to introduce air, yet limits the flow to a gradual trickle that allows you to control any sediment in the bottle. Some decanters have glass or metal closures that are used to hold the wine after it has been decanted. These should be used when tastings of the wine reveal that its complexity and flavor is at a peak to limit further air entering the beverage.

Before you decant, carefully and gently inspect your bottle of wine. Wine that has been aged for a number of years may contain a great deal of sediment or hardly any at all. A low-voltage light or a candle flame held behind the bottle will highlight the presence of any bottle sediment, allowing you to position the bottle for decanting and prevent the sediment from flowing into the decanter. In most cases, the wine's horizontal racking settles sediment on the bottle's side. Move the bottle gently to keep loose sediment from dislodging and clouding the wine.

Many aged red wines have enhanced flavor when they are decanted, but decant with caution. Some very old wines benefit from simple careful pouring that avoids transferring sediment to the glass, without the extra oxygenation of decanting. When decanting is necessary, it should be conducted in the presence of the taster after you present the bottle and open it [see Opening Wines, page 162].

Decanting of younger wines allows them to rapidly mature, as if it was cellared for years. This effect helps you determine the potential for aging in currently released wines.

Follow the steps and options shown to decant your bottle of fine red wine.

STEP 1

Following presentation of the bottle to the taster, gently bring the bottle to an upright position. Uncork the wine [see Opening Wines, page 162], disturbing the sediment in the bottle as little as possible. On aged bottles with older corks, hold the corkscrew's spiral near the cork as you withdraw it, then grasp the cork itself to prevent breakage.

UPRIGHT

UPRIGHT DECANTING Stand the bottle upright and allow its sediment to settle at the bottom of the bottle before following steps 1–3 above; allow at least a day for older red wines to settle, perhaps only a few hours for younger reds.

STEP 2

Clean the bottle neck and inside its lip, then gently rotate the bottle onto the side containing the greatest amount of sediment. Pour the wine slowly into the decanter. A straining sieve may be used to trap cork particles, but floating sediment in the wine should always remain below the liquid level of the bottle being poured.

STEP 3

Stop at the first sign that sedimentation is reaching the lip. Use the light of a candle, a low-wattage bulb, a flashlight, or other direct light source to observe movement of the sediment in the bottle as you pour the wine.

HORIZONTAL

HORIZONTAL DECANTING Use a wine cradle to transfer the bottle from the cellar, and avoid standing it upright at any time until the wine is decanted. The cradle will hold the bottle with ullage at the cork, allowing it to be opened.

STRAINING SIEVE

USING A STRAINER Use a clean, tightly-woven straining sieve to filter sediment as you decant wines such as port or sherry—but avoid their use with fine red wines. You'll capture most of the bottle's liquid while eliminating much of its dregs.

THE TASTING RITUAL

A wine tasting engages all of the senses to gain a full appreciation of your wine, as well as allowing you to discern between different wines you've chosen to taste. The tasting ritual is an opportunity to refine your senses and gain information about each bottle, rather than an opportunity to consume wine—you'll have ample opportunity to drink your wine once you have noted all of its attributes and chosen a favorite from the group.

Tasting wine is the fruit of your labor for the proper presentation, opening, and—if you wish—decanting of the beverage for your guests. It is the culmination of the wine-making and aging process, where years of effort and subtle development reach your nose and palate.

Before your guests arrive, rinse out with fresh water and carefully dry stemware appropriate for the grape varietals you plan to consume. Tastings should always be conducted with clean glasses free of residue from soap or a tasting of previous wine. If several wines will be tasted in sequence, provide a pitcher of water and a dregs container for your guests to clean their glasses or plan to replace the stemware with each new wine you serve.

Quality stemware should have a sharp, cut edge at the top of the bowl. The best stemware is crystal; it contains tiny imperfections that agitate the wine as you swirl it in the glass to improve aeration.

Grasp the glass with your fingers at its stem. Avoid holding its bowl in your palm; the heat from your hand will warm the glass and wine inside. Wines served at too cool a temperature can be rapidly warmed to a proper drinking temperature by cradling the glass in your palms.

Follow the steps shown in sequence to taste wine.

STEMWARE

Use clean stemware suited to the wine being tasted. Fill the glass with one to two ounces (three to six ml) of wine, to the bowl's widest point. Space permits swirling.

SMELL

Take a short, quick sniff the wine when it is freshly poured and again after swirling it in the glass. Is the wine's scent pleasant ? Does it smell of cork, vinegar, sulphur, or mold, or of fruit, earth, wood, or other pleasing aromas?

APPEARANCE

Hold the glass of wine to the light. Is it clear? Do you see bubbles on the glass or in the liquid? What is its hue? For white wines, note green tints; in reds, variation at the rim.

SIGHT

Swirl the wine. Note the "legs" that form on the bowl's sides; slow, thick legs reveal more alcohol than fast, thin ones. Deeply colored legs denote richness.

TASTE

Sip the wine. Curl it around your tongue. Move it from cheek to cheek to release its flavors. Draw in air through the liquid and note how its flavor changes. Note the wine's flavor, amount of tannin, acidity, sweetness, fullness, and balance.

AFTER TASTING

Empty your mouth—with or without swallowing—and consider the wine's aftertaste. Was the initial taste and aftertaste consistent with the wine's scent? Use a neutral cracker or bread to cleanse your palate before the next tasting.

PAIRING FOOD WITH WINE

Matching popular wine categories and specific foods can enhance your enjoyment of both the cuisine you are tasting and your wine.

Food and wine are fundamentally linked, far more than a simple lending of names to one or another culinary magazine devoted to the subject. Despite centuries of advice, however, pairing food with wine still seems mysterious for many people; one may be afraid to make a faux pas by serving the wrong wine with the right food, or vice versa.

Like discovering wines or foods you enjoy, pairing the two is an enjoyable journey of experimentation. General guidelines exist, but serve only as points of departure. The venerable "red wine with red meat, white with pork, chicken and fish" maxim still applies, but many cutting-edge chefs and sommeliers are now striking off in other directions.

Think beyond pairing a grape varietal with a main course. Your choice of wine might complement that course or another dish. Will a roast be finished with a wine-reduction sauce that adds the flavor of fruit to the meat? Consider a fruit-filled, rich wine to complement it. Avoid competing tastes, but consider a wine's character more than its color.

Shellfish such as mussels steamed in a broth of white wine, garlic, lemon, onion, and butter is a natural pairing for a dry white wine, such as a Chenin Blanc. The rich flavor also works with light, dry red wines.

Dry wines are often best served with the meal. Their high acidity helps cleanse the palate and strikes counterpoints to enrich the food's taste. Light wines tend to complement hors d'oeuvres, soups, salads, and lighter fare; by contrast, heavier wines are a preferred counterpart to foods with more assertive tastes. For example, a light, dry Chenin Blanc might improve a steamed or stir-fried vegetable dish, while a grilled or barbecued recipe might require a heartier-bodied dry red such as Pinot Noir. Sweet wines are often reserved for desserts.

Consider pairing a light-bodied, medium-tannin red wine with pork or veal. While it's true that a rich red varietal often complements meat dishes, the lighter reds also pair nicely with light-flavored meats, fowl, and cheese or sauced dishes such as poultry or vegetables. Reserve robust, rich reds for game birds and flavorful roasts or other red meat.

Similarly, food pairings with white wines vary. Light or dry varietals are best served alone, prior to or after the meal. A crisp wine with a light acid content would complement fish and light pasta dishes. Fruity, low-acid white wines tend to enrich sauced pasta, fish, and poultry, while whites with higher acidity can substitute for reds when you serve pork and veal. Rieslings, Pinot Gris, and Chenin Blancs hold their own with spicy, seasoned cuisines such as Mexican, Indian, Thai, and Vietnamese food.

Food and wine experts suggest focusing on a key ingredient such as a vegetable or sauce in the dishes you prepare as you select a wine to accompany a recipe. If you cook with wine, consider using wine of the same grape varietal with the meal.

While various wines complement many different foods, you'll be hard-pressed to match asparagus, most mustards, endives, radicchios, mints, and citrus fruits with a complementary wine. Chocolate also presents a challenge, though many connoisseurs enjoy it with port or Champagne and other dry, sparkling wines.

As you seek experience in the kitchen, use your wine collection to test these and other combinations. Who knows?—you might find the perfect match for an artichoke or horseradish right there in your cellar.

Matching a dessert wine with nuts, richly flavored cheeses, and tangy fruits is a sure ticket to bringing a meal to a satisfying close. Of all the wine rules you may hear, the one that always holds true is to avoid pairing wine with a food that is sweeter than the wine, since it makes the wine taste bitter.

AUTHOR'S ACKNOWLEDGEMENTS

I have been blessed with the ability to combine my work with what has become a passion of mine for nearly two decades. There have been many benefits associated with this business of building custom wine cellars, some of which are:

- the great people with whom I have been able to work over the years,
- the personally gratifying and rewarding projects I have had the pleasure to work on,
- the slight connection of mine to the wine industry.

This book would not have been possible without the help of Robert and Barbara Dolezal, whose fore sight and professionalism have contributed greatly to this project. Thanks also go to the book's principal photographer, John Rickard, for all the time and energy spent collecting photos and for making my wine cellars come to life. A special thanks to Rich Binsacca for all his efforts in helping to polish my thoughts.

And, of course, a thank you goes to my many clients who have allowed me to interrupt their busy lives to collect the photographs required for this book, especially the following:

- Chris Cartwright, Hussehn and Daniel Enan, John and Kathy Kehoe, Bill and Janet Kershaw, Barry and Valerie Krug, Dr. Darren and Pam Nills, Steve and Dana Olsen, Dennis and Toni Pierce, Jim and Kathy Skidmore, Kevin Stokke, and Mike and Bobbi Voris.
- Capitol Cellars (www.capitolcellars.com), (916) 786-9030
- The Kitchen Restaurant (www.thekitchenrestaurant.com), (916) 568-7171
- Vinotheque Wine Cellars (www.vinotheque.com), (800) 343-9463
- The Wine Consultant (www.thewineconsultant.com), (916) 721-WINE

Finally, a special thanks goes to my loving wife, Brenda, and our kids, Brooke and Scott, for putting up with my struggles to meet the ever-approaching deadline. I owe you for the time lost.

This acknowledgment would not be complete without saying thanks to Eric Stumpf, AKA The Wine Consultant; without his forethought, I might have never ventured into specializing in the strange yet wonderful business of wine cellar construction.

Perry Sims
www.simscellars.com

PHOTO CREDITS

All photographs by John M. Rickard, except for the following:

Jerry Bates: pgs. 78 (bot.), 79 (bot. left), 119 (bot. left & right), 149

E. Carey/The Cole Group ©1994: pg. 168

D. Fisher/ The Cole Group ©1994: pg. 13

F. Lyon/The Cole Group ©1994: pg. 169

James F. Wilson: pg. 29

PUBLISHER'S ACKNOWLEDGEMENTS AND RESOURCES

Drexel Heritage
4270 Rosewood Drive
Pleasanton, CA
Phone 925-847-7374

Pacific Union Homes and Mayfield Developers L.P.
Vineyard Gate
2675 St. Helena Court
Livermore, CA 94550
www.pacificunionhomes.com

Michael Pozzan
Pozzan Winery
Napa Valley CA
www.michaelpozzanwinery

Vino Cellars & Accessories
1772 First Street
Livermore, CA 94550
Phone 925-447-8000
www.vino-cellars.com

Graham Ball, Michael Patterson,
Jorge Tinoco, and Carolyn Wente
Wente Vineyards
5050 Arroyo Road
Livermore, CA 94550-9645
www.wentevineyards.com

WhisperKool
a division of Vinotheque Wine Cellars
(800) 343-9463
www.vinotheque.com

and the following individuals:

Lindsay Archer, Mt. Shasta, CA

Buzz Knight, Mt. Shasta, CA

Sblend A. Sblendorio, Livermore, CA

Scott Spruiell, Livermore, CA

Chris & Lori Tarantino, Livermore CA

INDEX